D0834177

# FROM
# MEMBERS

# TO
# DISCIPLES

# FROM MEMBERS

# TO DISCIPLES

## Leadership Lessons
## From the Book of Acts

### Michael W. Foss

Abingdon Press
*Nashville*

FROM MEMBERS TO DISCIPLES
LEADERSHIP LESSONS FROM THE BOOK OF ACTS

*This book is printed on acid-free paper.*

Library of Congress Cataloging-in-Publication Data

Foss, Michael W., 1948–
    From members to disciples: leadership lessons from the book of Acts / Michael W. Foss.
       p. cm.
    ISBN 978-0-687-46730-3 (binding: pbk., adhesive perfect : alk paper)
    1. Bible. N.T. Acts—Criticism, interpretation, etc. 2. Christian leadership. I. Title.

BS2625.6.L42F67 2007
253—dc22

                                                                            2006036987

07 08 09 10 11 12 13 14 15 16—10 9 8 7 6 5 4 3 2 1

MANUFACTURED IN THE UNITED STATES OF AMERICA

To the courageous disciples

who dare to believe

that the Holy Spirit

will renew Christ's church

for another century

# Contents

I. The Power of Waiting—Acts 1 . . . . . . . . . . . . . . . . . . . . . . . . . . . . 1

II. The Power of Passion—Acts 2 . . . . . . . . . . . . . . . . . . . . . . . . . . 11

III. The Power of Disciplined Growth—Acts 6 . . . . . . . . . . . . . . . . . 27

IV. An Unstoppable Power—Acts 8 . . . . . . . . . . . . . . . . . . . . . . . . . 49

V. The Power of Vision—Acts 16:6-10 . . . . . . . . . . . . . . . . . . . . . . 65

VI. The Power of Purpose—Acts 28 . . . . . . . . . . . . . . . . . . . . . . . . 87

# THE POWER OF WAITING——ACTS 1

## Introduction

Waiting has never been high on my priority list. I have found little or no mention of waiting as a critical function of leadership, but it is. Perhaps the real problem is that many of us confuse waiting with doing nothing. We don't understand how waiting can be an active, spiritual exercise in leadership. It is hard to imagine that waiting can be productive—but it can be. Effective leadership always begins with waiting.

> **Waiting is an active spiritual exercise of expectation.**

The first chapter of the Acts of the Apostles is a study on productive waiting. Luke writes:

> After his suffering he [Jesus] presented himself alive to them by many convincing proofs, appearing to them during forty days and speaking about the kingdom of God. While staying with them, he ordered them not to leave Jerusalem, but to wait there for the promise of the Father. "This," he said, "is what you have heard from me; for John baptized with water, but you will be baptized with the Holy Spirit not many days from now." (Acts 1:3-5)

The first great missional era of the Christian church began by wait-ing. Why? How would this season of waiting be productive? Why didn't

Jesus simply give the Holy Spirit at the moment of his ascension—
Acts 1:9?

We had just completed a major capital drive at Prince of Peace. One of
the key elements was the purchase of seven acres to the northwest of our
Worship Center. With the city of Burnsville, Minnesota, already built to
98 percent of its capacity, some of the few acres left for development were
just to the west of our property. I was aware that hotels and restaurants
had already made significant offers to the Fairview Hospitals and Clinics
real estate division that held title to the land. Abutted on the east and
south by three- to five-story buildings, with our northern boundary a
heavily traveled county road, the only hope for our church to have a
future with any visibility was for us to secure some of the property to our
west. Since we were part of a Planned Unit Development (PUD), green
space requirements and the necessity of sharing parking had previously
been determined. Those regulations allowed building to be developed up
to five stories high. If multi-storied buildings were placed directly to the
west, Prince of Peace would find itself at the bottom of a canyon.

We had received a letter of intent to sell seven acres to us. But, when
we went to finalize that agreement, things had changed on the hospital
side of things. With their need for expansion, simply selling us the land
was not in their best interest. The deal was off the table.

I waited. As conversations about the land deal plodded on and the
questions within the congregation grew more frequent, I could feel my
frustrations growing. What was God up to? Had I, or a member of our
team, dropped the ball? Why had this needed opportunity to secure our
future been lost? The weeks dragged on into months.

Then it happened. The conversation shifted to a land swap that was to
our benefit. There would not be any money spent from Prince of Peace.
Land that was not very useful to us but was very useful to the hospital
could be traded, and the parking lot we had added there would be pur-
chased by the hospital. More than that, for the first time in more than
thirteen years of my serving at Prince of Peace, there seemed to be the
possibility of the city vacating a street that ran between our Worship
Center and the land we would acquire. This would result in more available land to build upon than we had first thought possible, as well as
greater visibility for our ministry. While I had been impatiently struggling
against my waiting, God had been at work. As the hospital administrator
said, "God was working out a better deal for all of us."

We live in an Acts time. The enormous challenges before the
Protestant church in North America, when seen through the lens of the

Acts of the Apostles, become great opportunities for mission. The book of Acts serves as our playbook for ministry in this season of change and reformation. Why? Because the book of Acts reminds us of the presence and action of God in a time when we must learn new models and behaviors for effective ministry. This creative tension between trusting in the active presence of God through the Holy Spirit and a realistic understanding of the state of our churches is best presented in this first-century journal of our faith. This book also calls us back to discipleship as our model for ministry. We must go "back to the future"—and Acts proves remarkably helpful for twenty-first-century Christian leaders who want to move from the tired Membership Model of ministry to the Discipleship Model with all of its opportunities and challenges. Acts 1 tells us where and how to begin.

Leading congregations from the Membership Model into the Discipleship Model for ministry begins in waiting. The first chapter of Acts transforms waiting from a passive, frustrating experience into an active spiritual exercise of expectation. As leaders in ministry we are called to spiritual depth . . . and that begins in waiting. My failure to appreciate this lesson led to unnecessary

> As leaders in ministry we are called to spiritual depth . . . and that begins in waiting.

frustration and ineffective action. This failure was not the failure of vision or a lack of teamwork. It was, quite simply, a failure of faith.

The first key lesson in Acts 1 is a deepening of faith. We read: "*After his suffering he presented himself alive to them by many convincing proofs, appearing to them during forty days and speaking about the kingdom of God*" (v. 3).

Before the Holy Spirit would be sent, these leaders had to grow confident in their convictions. First, the Savior would convince them of his resurrection and the truth of the kingdom of God, and then they would meet together, sharing what they had seen and heard. This process built within each person a commitment to their mission as leaders. As that commitment galvanized, a sense of urgency emerged. (Surely this is a part of the question in verse 6.) As their urgency grew, the community experienced the power of obedience and prayer. Waiting is not a passive behavior for Christian leaders!

The Membership Model for ministry emerged in the aftermath of World War II in our country. As a consequence, we experienced significant growth across many denominations as this model for organizing and managing congregations standardized the administration, the exercise of ministry, the extension of missions beyond the local community, and the expectations of those who joined our churches. This success has proven short-lived, however. The Membership Model began to break down in the early 1970s. This breakdown became full-scale collapse in the mid-1980s.

This collapse was due to two significant factors. The first was that the model was not able to adapt to the changing expectations of a new generation. The baby boomer generation was much more participatory than their predecessors, the builder generation. This participation was not on an organizational level. Rather, this generation wanted to personally experience the various spiritual aspects, or practices, of the church—rather than support its institutional forms. The builder generation had experienced the rise of public institutions at an unprecedented pace. These institutions added significantly to the value and strength of American society. Committee structures, for example, created change. But the boomer generation had grown suspicious of institutions as self-serving expressions of the past. (This skepticism continues in the following generations as well.) A more immediate need for a personal engagement of the heart, as well as the need for direct evidence of a positive social impact from our institutions was required. But the Membership Model provided little for either of these changing expectations. A thirty-five-year-old leader in a congregation put it bluntly, "Why would I join a committee? A committee is a group of people who get together, talk a lot, and don't do anything."

The second significant factor for the collapse of the Membership Model for our ministries has been a change in meaning of the term "membership." Membership carried with it both an expectation of privilege as well as responsibility for previous generations. But in twenty-first-century United States, membership brings privilege with little or no responsibility. I become a "member" of Sam's Club and for a minimal fee I receive the benefits of discount purchases of large quantities of goods. Membership in the United States has come to mean minimal investment for maximum benefit. No wonder many committed pastors and lay leaders experience the church as a high demand, low support organization. The stated expectation of many churchgoers is that the pastor is "hired" by the church to be a personal or family chaplain and spiritual caregiver. Beyond that, the pastor and congregational leaders ought to keep the members happy by maintaining the comfort of those present and bringing new members in who can embrace and support what is already present.

Personal benefit has replaced evangelical mission. The status quo has supplanted productive change. Membership has replaced discipleship.

# The Promise of Purpose

The Discipleship Model for ministry begins, not with the promise of benefits, but with the promise of purpose. Disciples are gathered in community for mission. This is the purpose that is at the heart of what it is to be a unique expression of the Christian church. Individual Christians are invited into following Jesus Christ with a two-fold promise: eternal life that gives purpose to this life. The radical call of discipleship is to discover the power of giving to and participating in the work of God in our world.

Organizationally, disciple-making ministries are organic. The committee structure is replaced by teams of disciples engaged in advancing the mission by doing ministry. Gifts-based ministry transforms the task of caregiving from the job of a pastor to the call of spiritually gifted and trained lay ministers. The pastor is not the personal or family chaplain; the congregation becomes a community of care. The pastor and staff become equippers for God's gifted and called people to more effectively engage in the ministry of the kingdom of God. The expectations of disciples are clarified and simplified: to be in a living relationship with Jesus Christ, to meet him in worship and personal practices of the faith, and to be in a community of living witnesses to his life-giving presence in our world. The Membership Model is turned upside down. The forms of the church serve the function of the spiritual life and growth of disciples who take the gospel into our world in word and deed.

In the face of these realities, it becomes clear that a Spirit-led renewal of the ministry of our churches will begin with productive waiting. Leaders will need to grow deep in their commitment to the vision of the Discipleship Model for congregational ministry. Without this deeply embedded commitment to a new model for ministry, the conflict that always accompanies change will be difficult to face, let alone overcome.

We can imagine those first disciples gathering together and telling stories of the Lord. Their stories of faith would support one another. A growing conviction and excitement for the proclamation of Jesus as the Risen Messiah emerged. With that, a language with which to communicate that message could be developed. The first disciples of Jesus were growing in their waiting.

# Our First Task Is to Be Disciples

As we lead from the Membership Model of ministry into the Discipleship Model for ministry, our first task is to be disciples. We cannot possibly share what we are not and have not experienced ourselves. These first disciples would give what they had first received. Their identities had been forged through the events of that first holy week. This was not something they simply agreed with—this was the message of what they had already become. Disciple leaders will need to commit to their own practice of discipleship before striving to guide a congregation into a new model for ministry.

The next strategy for leading congregations into the renewal of ministry, that the Discipleship Model can provide, is for us to form a guiding coalition to share our hopes and dreams with one another. These hopes and dreams will emerge into mission and vision. In Luke's mind, these early disciples had been taught by the Risen One and had received his command: "*Thus it is written, that the Messiah is to suffer and to rise from the dead on the third day, and that repentance and forgiveness of sins is to be proclaimed in his name to all nations, beginning from Jerusalem*" (Luke 24:46-47). Now, on the other side of his ascension, their waiting was going to be a season of preparation and growth in order to fulfill that command in the power of the Holy Spirit.

# If Our Church Could Become an Acts Church, What Would It Look Like?

Gather a small group of leaders together with you. Begin in the Scriptures and prayer. Then ask the simple question: If our church could become an Acts church, what would it look like? What would Jesus Christ call us to be in this place and time? What would we do as a consequence? Pray together for the leading of the Holy Spirit and the timing only God can provide.

As you are growing with your leaders, invite them to begin the process of creating the new church. At Prince of Peace, we think of "icebergs." Icebergs have only ten percent of their mass above the water's surface. Ninety percent of the mass of the iceberg is invisible. So, we think of each visible leader as the tip of the iceberg. Each leader is to connect and recruit a team to work and grow with her or him. That means that, if you have a group of twelve, you will be creating a group that will expand to over one hundred. Each of these will be in a discipleship relationship with the leaders whom you are discipling. This pattern can be replicated as the question is asked again and again. The answers will create buy-in and increase the energy for mission. Accountability is to the vision and will develop boundaries as you come to understand your mission in your particular context.

Then wait and watch with expectation. Expect that God will be at work to "make a better deal" than you could have imagined.

# Invitation to Adventure

The second thing that this text teaches us about discipleship leadership is that the disciples didn't know everything. *"They asked him [Jesus], 'Lord, is this the time when you will restore the kingdom to Israel?' He replied, 'It is not for you to know the times or periods that the Father has set by his own authority'"* (Acts 1:6-7).

The invitation is to an adventure. Adventures promise many things, but certainty about everything is not one of them. Many leaders assume that there is a blueprint for disciple-making ministry that can simply be applied to their own circumstances. But leadership in the twenty-first century is always contextual. Each of us will learn what we need to know as we do it. That's why a community of committed leaders is so critical. As we learn together we grow together. As we grow together, we support one another and hold each other accountable to our mission—not to perfect implementation of that mission.

I was invited into their home in order to help plan her funeral. She had been diagnosed with a cancer that, against all odds, had been virulent and unabated. But she was a disciple—a follower of Jesus. We spoke of our faith and the confidence we share in the promise of life eternal. We also spoke of what we didn't know—when and how she would die, when this loving couple would see each other in eternity, and how her family would do without her. We shared that we didn't know everything, but we did know what matters.

The Discipleship Model for ministry acknowledges that we cannot know all we need to know, but we do know whose we are and who we are. We know what is essential. From that foundation of confidence, we can move into a future worthy of our living it. Congregations have been stuck in a glorious past without the hope of a future of God's making. The Discipleship Model expects to meet the Holy Spirit in our ministry—today and tomorrow.

As we wait, we pray. The followers of Jesus returned to Jerusalem, and Luke tells us, "*All these were constantly devoting themselves to prayer, together with certain women, including Mary the mother of Jesus, as well as his brothers*" (Acts 1:14). Prayer transforms our waiting into an active exercise of faith. Prayer is not the last thing disciples do—it is the first thing we do. Prayer opens our waiting to the power of God at work within and among us. In speaking of congregational change, one leader cautioned, "Move only as fast as you can on your knees." He was reminding us to pray first and then act.

# The Necessary Infrastructure

Out of this praying, sharing, learning time of waiting will emerge the next steps. The surprise in Acts 1 is that the first activity of this gathered community of faith was to put the infrastructure in place by the election of a twelfth disciple. The organization of the community would serve the witness of the community. The twelfth disciple was necessary in order for the witness of the first church to have biblical integrity. The new people of God would reflect God's actions in forming the first people of God. Just as Israel was formed of twelve tribes, so the new people of God would have twelve apostles. This continuity, not with the form but with the design of God, was essential in establishing an inner integrity.

Discipleship Model congregations will shape themselves around their best understanding of a New Testament model for ministry. Whatever organizational plan that requires, in any given setting, there are some clearly identifiable elements of the model.

First, it will be led by a leadership team of mature disciples. Second, it will be gifts-based ministry. Third, it will be designed for the best and quickest deployment of Gods' people in ministry within and beyond the congregation. Fourth, it will recognize that its authority before the world is in the Bible—not in its institutional identity. Last, it will be a people of prayer and active engagement in the world.

Let the institution be shaped by its mission. Only in this way will our churches be churches . . . and not clubs.

In electing Matthias as the twelfth disciple, the early Christian community recognized the mission and witness of the church as definitive of its structure. As disciple-making ministry emerges within a congregation, changes will be required in the organization of that particular ministry. Allow the emergent church to lead to these changes. First, wait on the commands of Christ, through prayer and scripture reading; then, as this renewal becomes visible and gains momentum, make the necessary changes.

Some suggest that electing Matthias was an act of impatience. The twelfth disciple would be chosen by the Holy Spirit—and it would be Saint Paul. In the early Christian community's eagerness to prepare for the work of Christ, they acted without waiting and chose one who would not be a significant witness to the Resurrection. After all, apart from this single reference, who ever heard of Matthias?

Disciple-making leaders understand that, if that was the case, it is an affirmation of productive waiting. Regardless of which particular understanding of Acts 1 we have, the infrastructure that will be blessed by the Holy Spirit (as identified throughout the book of Acts) will have mission at its core. As we shall see, the organization of the church in the book of Acts will change as the mission evolves and moves into new contexts and times.

# Questions and Reflections

1. How have you experienced waiting as a key leadership activity? Reflect on a time of productive waiting in your ministry or life of faith. What did you do to make your season of waiting worthwhile? How did your faith grow—or did it? Would you be willing to share your story with another person of faith and then invite them to share such a story with you?

2. What are the important lessons for your context from Acts 1?

3. If you do not have a small group for prayer and study in order to discern how best to lead your congregation into God's future, how might you form one?

4. Is your congregation aware of and committed to its mission? Are you structured to achieve that mission?

5. What future for your ministry is so great that only God could do it?

I I

# THE POWER OF PASSION—ACTS 2

## The Right Time and Place

Timing is everything. How often have we heard that or said it? And we know that it is true. On the one hand, we have watched as an athlete rises to the occasion at just the right moment to lead her or his team to a stunning victory. Or, we have listened as a musician instinctively moves through a piece and, at just the right moment, increases the tempo or dramatically changes the volume in the performance.

On the other hand, we have also seen teams who have had the advantage suddenly sag and lose their momentum. They look and feel as though they have run out of gas and have spent their energy and focus too early. The outcome is unavoidable. And we have watched as actors have carried a character too far for too long. What had been interesting becomes farcical or, worse yet, boring.

In ministry, timing is equally important. When a leader or a group of leaders are called to help a congregation move from fixation on the past or ineffectiveness in the present, we need to pay attention to our timing. But how do we discern the right time? There are no graphs that can pinpoint the perfect moment. There is no formula for figuring out when just the right time will occur for God's people to move into the future.

Acts 2 is all about God's timing. Having waited in prayer, the followers of Jesus had grown deeply. They had surely shared their stories and reflected on the teachings of the Savior. As they waited, their inner urgency must have grown. As they waited, God was creating a heavenly

11

convergence of circumstance and religious fervor outside of that upper room. God's timing would prove to be perfect. We read:

> When the day of Pentecost had come, they [all the believers] were all together in one place. And suddenly from heaven there came a sound like the rush of a violent wind, and it filled the entire house where they were sitting. Divided tongues, as of fire, appeared among them, and a tongue rested on each of them. All of them were filled with the Holy Spirit and began to speak in other languages, as the Spirit gave them ability. (Acts 2:1-4)

Those first followers of Jesus had been waiting. Because of the promise of the Savior that they would receive the gift from God of the Holy Spirit, their waiting had been transformed into anticipation. Now that anticipation would be fulfilled. This great gift would push the church from a small group of individuals who had privatized the message of the resurrection into a dynamic movement of believers whose faith became very public indeed! The gift of tongues and the rushing of a wind (surely the identifying mark of the Spirit's presence) must have been overwhelming. But these gifts, as dramatic as Luke presents them to us, are not the point. The point is that the gifts—all signs of the promised Holy Spirit—serve a greater purpose than simply energizing those who had been waiting. That purpose was to actively enter into the mission of God.

"How many of you have ever stopped your business and planning sessions in order to pray and ask what God would have you do? How many of you have asked, not what the pastor thought, or the church council, or even what you might have thought, but what God was calling you to in the future?" I asked. As I raised my hand in invitation, no others raised theirs. "Raise your hand if you have done this," I said. **And not a single hand went up.**

It was in Baltimore, Maryland, and I was standing before a group of nearly 500 congregational leaders. Pastors, lay staff members, and non-staff leaders of many churches were present. Some were church council members. Others were leaders of particular ministries within their congregations. I am not sure how that moment came, but I remember it very clearly. It was as if the idea that God might have a purpose for the future ministry of a congregation had never occurred to any of them. How remarkable!

12

Isn't this the question that sets the church apart from being a club? Isn't this the claim of faith that changes our business into mission? And if God isn't calling us into the future, what's the point?

I was not suggesting that planning and the execution of ministry by our disciple-members is not important. Nor was I suggesting that praying about God's purpose will cause a blueprint to float down from heaven. I was, and am, suggesting that the power of prayer can both open us to God's leading through the Holy Spirit and clarify our direction. And this can happen at any level or area within our congregations.

There is nothing in this text that suggests that only the Twelve received the power and leading of the Holy Spirit. In fact, Luke writes: "They were **all** together in one place" (Acts 2:1, emphasis added). In Acts 1 this included men and women and, with the election of Matthias, it is clear that many more than the Twelve and a few significant women were there. All of them received the gift of the Holy Spirit. All of them were energized for mission through the speaking in other languages—"as the Spirit gave them ability" (Acts 2:4).

The first heavenly convergence of God's timing began in the experience of the community gathered. Leaders in ministry will learn that we can test the timing of God by first, praying for God to show us when the right time is. Then, we watch and listen for the signs of the Spirit's activity within the community. This isn't waiting for consensus. Rather, it is sensing when the missional moment has come. Acts 2:1-4 describes the first half of a missional moment.

# Missional Moments

The first part of any missional moment is the release of energy (wind) combined with the language of discipleship (tongues). If there is no energy among a significant number of the disciples gathered together and no common expression of purpose, the missional moment has not come. Leaders in the

> When there is energy among a significant number of the disciples gathered together and a common expression of purpose, the missional moment has come.

13

twenty-first-century church strive to build energy by turning the attention of our members into the future that discipleship promises. With that will come a common language for personal and congregational spiritual growth and, out of that, clarity of purpose. When a significant number— not all!—of the gathered people of God show the presence of these two aspects of faith, then the missional moment has arrived. The leader(s) will then need to identify that and move outward in specific and identifiable acts of mission.

The second part of any missional moment is found in Acts 2:5-13:

> Now there were devout Jews from every nation under heaven living in Jerusalem. And at this sound the crowd gathered and was bewildered, because each one heard them speaking in the native language of each. Amazed and astonished, they asked, "Are not all these who are speaking Galileans? And how is it that we hear, each of us, in our own native language?" . . . All were amazed and perplexed, saying to one another, "What does this mean?" But others sneered and said, "They are filled with new wine."

While God had been preparing the inner life of the believers for the gift of the Holy Spirit, God also had created a heavenly convergence of opportunity outside the church. The festival of Pentecost was a pilgrimage festival. Those who came were devout Jews with a passion for their faith. At just the right time a multitude of nationalities and ethnicities were gathered where they could receive the witness of those first followers of Jesus. The disciples were now prepared to give the news of Jesus' resurrection, and the "crowd" was made up of people whose religious passion would have prepared many of them to receive that witness. It was the right time for the right witness to the right people.

Six years ago, we at Prince of Peace experienced a remarkable phenomenon. Suddenly, people offered us furniture to be given to those who needed it. We had no furniture ministry at the time, but our director of mission accepted the first piece with the confidence that someone could be found who needed it. The next day a family called asking for those very pieces of furniture. Over the next few weeks we experienced this occurrence again and again. Sometimes it was the donation of some nice furniture (we would not accept furniture that was in bad shape) that, within a day or two, would be requested by a family unknown to us. Sometimes it was a request by a family or individual for furniture we didn't have—and within forty-eight hours those pieces would simply show up. Last year more than 5,000 pieces of furniture were delivered or given away by more than 100 volunteers led by two part-time staff members. More than that, this ministry has grown into a food pantry and clothes closet that has served nearly 1,000 families—many of whom have small children.

The missional moment had arrived. The hearts of the disciples at Prince of Peace were open to serve a population we had not served before and in a manner we had never imagined. And the community had grown in ways that prepared our greater community to receive this ministry. And with each delivery or gift of food or clothing a Bible is offered, and prayers surround it.

How do leaders know when God's timing has come? We look for the energy and language of discipleship within our churches, and then we watch for a missional opportunity that only God could create. Then, leaders lead—into God's future.

Too often, however, our congregations function from a vision that is limited to the past or to what we think can happen. The first sign that a church has outlived its vision for ministry is when there is little passion left for mission. Tragically, the only passion that seems to come is most often centered in conflict or resistance to change.

Not long ago I prayed with a pastor and two of his congregational leaders. My prayer was for courage and a "thick skin." His United Methodist church had an older worshiping membership that had decreased to between fifty and seventy per week. But the community was changing. Young people were moving into the neighborhood. Some visited his church and left. Others stayed—and brought a new energy to lackluster areas of ministry like the children's ministry. He and his leaders had grown excited about a Discipleship Model for their ministry. But some of the "older members" were not only challenging this new development but also saying vile things about him and his leadership.

Amazing—the congregation appeared to have no viable future without a significant change of both direction (vision) and organization, but some would rather have the congregation die than change. In all fairness, they had achieved their initial vision decades ago. But, rather than cast a new vision for this new time, some preferred to hang on to the "glory days" of their past.

In situations like that, pastors and leaders have the obligation to ask if this is the call of God or not. The call of God to each of us is worth our living it. This is both simple and true. God never calls an individual, family, or church into a life that is not worthy of their living and giving for it. In our time, we have seen more and more clergy, from all denominations, answer this question by leaving the church.

This pastor, however, had a growing group of leaders within the congregation who shared his passion for mission and were willing to help move the church ahead. When I asked if it was time for him to consider a new congregation, he was shocked and strongly affirmed his ongoing commitment to this congregation. That's when we prayed for courage, strength, and that God would either change the hearts of his critics or help them go someplace where they could be spiritually satisfied and fed.

The energy within his congregation was not from the past. It was growing among both new and older members of his church. They were praying for a new day of effective ministry beyond themselves. The age of Acts had arrived.

# Not Everyone Will Make It

But just as with the advent of the Holy Spirit, its evidence in Acts 2 was not welcomed by all, so Spirit-led and missional ministry will not be affirmed by everyone. Yes, many of those who heard were engaged and wondered how it could be and what it meant. But there were those who scoffed. (Luke's language is dramatic: "*But others sneered . . .*")

The power of the Membership Model is that it is comfortable. This is what most of us have been raised with and what most pastors have been trained for. This is the model that led to a time of church expansion and the formation of denominations that impacted the world. But the model has lost its ability to impact a new age. Leaders of disciple-making ministries will understand that discomfort is rarely welcomed within the church. It is only natural that criticism and conflict (scoffing) will occur as we strive to lead an effective congregation.

> Missional moments are not without conflict, but they are God's open doorway into a viable future for ministry.

Membership Model ministries frequently suffer from an addiction to what is "reasonable." Many great opportunities in ministry have been lost because the possibilities seemed too "unreasonable" to be acted upon. This doesn't mean that we should not take a clear assessment of our resources and our context. But if that is all we do, then we are not open to the God of impossible possibilities. It would have been reasonable to have refused those first few donations of furniture—and it crossed our minds! After all, we had no ministry in place to handle them and give them away. But God was leading us into an "unreasonable" possibility that was just beyond our imaginations.

**When faced with the challenge that a ministry opportunity is unreasonable, invite the church to pray that God will open or close the doors to this ministry.** Then wait and watch to see how God lines up your circumstances. The greatest visions have always begun with the first step— doing what God sets before us. Then, prayerfully, we look to see where that obedient response leads us. Sometimes, that is all that we can do. More often than not, however, the first step is over the threshold of mission that God has set before us—we just couldn't see it. Arguments about what is reasonable or not ought to be taken seriously and need to be taken to God in prayer—not just accepted as fact.

The point is that missional moments are not without conflict. But they are God's open doorway into a viable future for our ministries. This emergence of the Christian witness at Pentecost was the result of the growth of a community of faith that could encourage and uphold those who would emerge as the leaders of this movement. Effective Discipleship Model leaders will not lead alone but will be surrounded by a group of prayerful, like-minded, and impassioned sister and brother disciples.

God's gift of the Holy Spirit led to the first public proclamation of the gospel, according to Luke. What can we learn from this sermon? Surely Luke has something in mind with the structure and content of Peter's message. The question of whether it actually happened this way—after all, who was taking notes?—is beside the point. The real emphasis is how this can be another part of the blueprint for twenty-first-century Christian leadership.

# Peter's Sermon

We had come together at a pastors' conference to meet with our bishop at that time, Bishop Cliff Lunde. We met in Woodburn, Oregon, and Bishop Lunde led our worship. The sermon was one of the best I have ever heard. Bishop Lunde reflected on Ephesians 6:12—"*For our struggle is not against enemies of blood and flesh, but against the rulers, against the authorities, against the cosmic powers of this present darkness, against the spiritual forces of evil in the heavenly places.*" Then he went on to say that, as pastors we should always remember that people are never the enemy. People may serve the enemy or be dupes of the enemy. But they are never the enemy.

I got it! I was struggling at the time with conflict in my congregation. We were expanding, and some of those who were joining our church didn't share the agenda of those who were already there. The consequence was a struggle over what ministries we would do and in what order. Good people were behaving badly, . . . but they were not the enemy.

The power of that sermon was the combination of the right words at the right time in my life. The Holy Spirit used them to open my eyes to a different way of seeing the conflict that always emerges when congregations undergo change. So, I usually take the conflicts less personally than I did. I rarely identify persons as the real problem or "enemy." And I always ask if the conflict is a spiritual correction for me or if it is a testimony to our forward progress.

# Context, Content, and Consequence

The first Christian sermon in Acts 2 is in three parts: Context, Content, and Consequence.

The context for this sermon is the reaction of the crowd that had gathered in response to the tumult of the Spirit's arrival. The message in Acts 2 begins where the listeners are. Their interest and questions set the stage for Peter's sermon. Notice how Luke records Peter addressing both the wonder and the skepticism of the crowd. In so doing, he acknowledges that what they are seeing and hearing is extraordinary.

We read: "*Men of Judea and all who live in Jerusalem, let this be known to you, and listen to what I say. Indeed, these are not drunk, as you suppose, for it is only nine o'clock in the morning. NO, this is what was spoken through the prophet Joel*" (vv. 14-16, emphasis added).

In the twenty-first century, preaching must be different. From the beginning of the settlement of our continent and the rise of the United States, we could most often assume a certain level of biblical literacy. This might be in the form of learned Bible stories. It might be in the form of persons who read and remember biblical teaching. Or, it would have been in the public expression of politicians and other civil leaders.

We now live in an age of biblical illiteracy. At Prince of Peace we are discovering that many of our worshipers don't even know that there are two testaments or parts to the Christian Bible—let alone how they fit together. The names and places in the Bible are foreign and often hard to pronounce. The connection between an Old Testament lesson and the Gospel lesson is often vague and the point in using them side-by-side is lost on the hearer. Worship seems cluttered with words that have meaning only to the "insiders." Like those who first heard the eruption of sound and language on that first Pentecost, the visitors to our churches increasingly hear words that may seem familiar but what they mean is another story entirely. Worship, one of the great practices of our faith, is confusing and without value.

This has led to a great opportunity. Our worship events now focus on a single theme that is set forth in song, response reading, Bible reading and preaching. One Bible passage is preached upon. The emphasis is on application of the biblical truths that passage sets before us. This simplifying of the message has led to a greater desire for biblical teaching as well as a reappraisal of the authority of the Scripture for the life of each worshiper. The messages may sound simplistic, but the intent is to take seriously the context of our worshipers' lives. We want to ask not only, "What does the Bible say?" but also, "Why does it say it, and what does that mean for you and me?"

We often begin with questions—or we introduce them later in the sermon. Recently in reflecting on Luke 24 and Jesus' appearance after the resurrection, I began with the question: Is this real? I then moved through other often-heard questions about the resurrection. The model that is used at Prince of Peace is from Peter's sermon. Context for our message is critical.

We all know that. The problem is that we are so used to a particular form of worship and preaching that it is difficult to reassess our context for ministry. But our understanding of our context will often determine if the content of our message will have any meaning to our hearers. The context is changing so rapidly in our time

**Understanding our context can determine if the content of our message will have any meaning to our hearers.**

that just ten years can make a great deal of difference. For example, ten years ago our context was Caucasian American, third-ring suburb. Burnsville understood itself as a bedroom community to the Twin Cities, particularly Minneapolis. But today, this area has become a global microcosm. Our neighbors today might be African American, Somali, Eastern European, first-generation immigrants from Asia, and Latinos and Latinas. In the past ten years the world moved into Burnsville, Minnesota!

This change in context is shaping our message and ministry. Spanish has become the second language of our outreach ministry. Our young people have a global mentality—not only through the Internet but also through their friends at school. How we preach the gospel requires a global awareness that was simply not a part of the equation just ten years ago.

Peter read his context very well. His sermon is a response to the real questions of real people. What would the real questions of our neighbors be? How can we learn what they are?

One of my personal mission fields is a Starbuck's not far from the church. The staff and customers have come to know me there. I have been asked to step outside by both in order to respond to the real-life issues of young people who haven't been to church in years—if ever. What a great opportunity to listen and learn.

# Where Is Your Listening Post?

In your area there are listening posts that you can identify. What might they be? How might you interact and build relationships with those who are not a part of your church or any church at all? The better we understand our larger community context, the more effective our message will be—just like this sermon in Acts 2.

The content of the gospel, in terms of language and use of the biblical narrative, emerges out of our mission context. In twenty-first-century America, the context for effective proclamation is relationships. Discipleship ministry is all about relationships.

> Discipleship ministry is all about relationships.

For Peter, the content of his sermon would connect with a pilgrim people alive in the passion of their faith and the hope of the Messiah.

Peter's relationship with his hearers would have been natural. But he intentionally builds upon this relationship by connecting with their understanding of the world. Instead of simply saying that they were seeing and hearing the power of God's Spirit at work, Peter links this extraordinary event to the prophecy of Joel. This leads to the witness to Jesus and his resurrection—which Peter again places within the context of God's design through the witness of Scriptures.

The point is two-fold. First, Peter wants to make it absolutely clear that we do not worship a capricious God. What has happened in Jesus of Nazareth, what is happening among this group of people in this outburst in Jerusalem, is all part of God's faithfulness. God is keeping the promises made to God's people, and they are invited to participate in it.

The second point is that the authority of Peter's witness is neither in the event itself nor in Peter himself. The authority of his word is in the word of God.

# Authority in Our Witness

In twenty-first-century America, the church has no authority in itself. Unlike a time, not long ago, when the church as a valued institution of society could speak and expect to be heard, today we are met with confusion or skepticism. The authenticity of the Christian message has been compromised by well-publicized moral failure among our leaders. We receive more publicity when our voices are strident than when they are reconciling. And, as the culture has continued to change, we can be easily dismissed as arcane.

Leading from membership to discipleship requires a reappraisal of how we say what we say. When we presume to have a right to be heard as an institution, present generations tend to more easily ignore us. But the regard for the Bible and its authority in spiritual matters remains high. More importantly, when leaders base their messages on the Bible it lends an authenticity to our words because people consider that we ought to be speaking from that perspective. As our context has continued to rapidly change, our content has grown closer to God's word. What has changed is not the source of our words but the connection to real life that we must now make more intentionally.

Peter makes the inherent connections between the Scriptures and the hearer's context overt. Notice how he does this. It is as if he were saying,

"Your perceptions of the event before you are accurate. But your conclusions aren't. This isn't chaos or new wine, it is the fulfillment of God's promise. And, by the way, the recent events concerning Jesus of Nazareth—they are accurate as well. But what God was doing was something other than what you thought. And what you were doing was not what you thought either. So, change your hearts and minds! This Jesus who seemed to you to be a charlatan, was, in fact, the Messiah—and Scripture affirms this."

Twenty-first-century preachers and teachers of the Christian message will learn from this sermon. We must take what we believe to be inherent in the word of God and make it crystal clear. The context requires an application that is overt. This is our content.

By the way, if you want an example that is in marked contrast to this effective message, read Acts 17. There Paul will attempt to communicate to the philosophers gathered at the Areopagus in Athens. Paul will combine rabbinic Mishnah (sermon) with Stoic philosophy, as a presentation of the gospel, and entirely miss his audience. The relationship between the preacher and the listeners is missing. Paul's lack of understanding of his context will lead him to misread the multiplicity of idols for a spiritual passion. At the Areopagus, intellectual distance and the exchange of ideas *as ideas* will take the place of religious fervor.

The point is that discipleship leaders have the responsibility of accurately reading where "point A" is with their community and people. To misread, as Paul does in Acts 17, is to mishandle a remarkable opportunity. The truth is that most religious leaders assume "point A" is much further down the road in terms of theological interest or understanding than it

## Acts time is a pre-Christian Age.

really is. If we live in an Acts time, then we live in a **pre-Christian Age.** Our worship and preaching will need to back up and start where people really are, not where we would like them to be, in order to experience the transformational consequences of the Holy Spirit.

# Power Surge

When we wanted to help the disciple-members of Prince of Peace remember the practices around which our discipleship ministry would be organized, for example, the phrase *POWER SURGE* emerged. Each of the consonants represents one of our Six Marks of Discipleship. So, P reminds us of the practice to *Pray daily*; W calls us to *Worship weekly*; R invites us into God's word by *Reading the Bible daily*; S stands for *Serving in and beyond the congregation*; the second R calls us to *Relate to others for spiritual growth*; and the G is our call to *Give a tithe and beyond*.

The R for *Relate to others for spiritual growth* has had a significant but unpredicted consequence in the lives of some of our disciples. Originally it was intended to call us into small groups. But, as one disciple told me, "Now that I get that second 'R' I can't treat my colleagues at work the same way I used to. Each of us is spiritual. That means that God values and gifts everyone."

When we see others as spiritual persons, we open ourselves to the call of the Holy Spirit to reach out with the hope and joy of our faith. It is less easy to dismiss another person or their ideas. We can't categorize others so quickly. Our work will also result in an environment change—as my friend found. Leading from membership into discipleship creates a set of expectations that many of us find empowering. We can no longer leave our faith in church or at home. Disciple-making ministries intentionally intrude on the lives of believers in Jesus' name. The everyday interactions we have with our co-workers or that weird neighbor next door subtly change over time.

The content of our preaching is centered in Jesus—his life, death, and resurrection—and the promises he gives to all who believe. But such preaching in the power of the Holy Spirit expects consequences to occur. I have learned to make such outcomes in the lives of disciples obvious. I will often speak directly to teens and apply the message to specific behaviors they can implement at school or in their relationships. I also will call adults to convert the ideas of the Scripture as presented in the sermon into behaviors.

I was entering the grocery store when I heard a van's horn honk, and the van pulled up next to me. "Thank you, Pastor Mike, for the challenge in yesterday's sermon. I have already acted on the first one, and we're talking about the second action you challenged us to take," the lady said, with a nod to her husband who was driving. "If you hadn't challenged us, we'd never have thought of doing what we just did—and I love it!"

The sermon had been on the power of love to create life choices in our lives. The love of God (*agape*) is an active and sacrificial love that has little or nothing to do with liking someone or how we feel. It is the external expression of an internal commitment to follow the commands of Christ.

That's when I challenged the congregation to join me in three specific actions the coming week. First, I challenged each person to find a need, no matter how small, and just meet the need with a concrete act of kindness. Second, I shared that my wife and I would be giving a sacrificial, financial gift this week above our tithing and I challenged each person to give such a financial gift as an expression of God's love in their lives—whether or not that gift came to Prince of Peace was beside the point. And last, I urged each person to connect with a friend—especially one that they hadn't seen in awhile—and give the gift of time to that friendship. Obviously, for at least one family those challenges were heard, and they were committed to responding to each one in the coming week.

This shouldn't surprise us! Peter's sermon created a tangible outcome: "*So those who welcomed his message were baptized, and that day about three thousand persons were added*" (Acts 2:41).

The tragedy of much of Christian preaching is that both the preacher and the hearer have no expectation that their lives will change as a consequence of the message! The most that many of us as preachers hope is to change a person's mind about something. While that may be an appropriate goal at times, it falls far short of the expectations of preaching in the New Testament—and especially in the book of Acts. The proclamation of the gospel in Acts *creates* change. That change can be positive, as in Acts 2, or it can be resisted and erupt in conflict. But the assumption of the book of Acts is that Christian preaching *does something* in and through the hearers.

> **The proclamation of the gospel in Acts *creates* change.**

# The Invitation of Christian Faith

The invitation of the Christian faith is not to come and consider a few good ideas but, through faith, to receive a great life. Disciples understand the power of the Holy Spirit as God's gift to transform our convictions into life choices. We know the grace of God is there for us, just as it was for those first hearers in Acts 2. Forgiveness is a new beginning when we have fallen short. So this is not about perfection but about a living faith. Christian preaching trusts the Holy Spirit to act and accomplish what only God can do.

Often before worship the worship team of vocalists, musicians, and pastors, will gather at the front for prayer. When I have prayed I have intentionally asked God to help us do the best we can in leadership *so that* we get out of the way and let God do what only God can do. Our striving for excellence in worship is our way of giving the best we have to God. But we fully understand that any real outcome in the lives of people through our worship will be the work of the Holy Spirit. The consequence is that we expect transformation to happen—in God's way and time.

# Questions and Reflections

1. Reflect on a time when you were moved in worship. What happened? Did it have any lasting impact on your life?

2. Have you ever heard a sermon that stayed with you for a long time? What was said, and why do you think it had such an impact on you?

3. What would happen if the pastor and the people gathered in worship prayed and expected that the Holy Spirit would show up? Is such transformational expectation a part of your worship life?

4. Have you met someone for whom life-change has been a significant part of that person's experience of faith? How do you respond to his or her story?

5. Would you consider meeting with the pastor and music leaders to pray for the Holy Spirit to use your worship for spiritual transformation?

6. Pastor, would you consider including challenges as a regular part of your sermons? Why? Why not?

# THE POWER OF DISCIPLINED GROWTH—ACTS 6

## The Crisis of Success

"Ninety-nine percent of the problems and conflicts in organizations are systems errors," I said. "The problem is that in the church we almost always assume someone has made a mistake. We look for someone to blame. Unfortunately, we can usually find someone. But when we place the blame there we rarely go any further and look into the system that created the problem. But if our first assumption is that the problem is a systems error and pursue it from

> **Always assume it's a systems problem first.**

that perspective, if it really is an individual's shortcoming, we'll find it. Always assume it's a systems problem, because if it is a problem person, that will surface. But it is most frequently not anyone's fault."

The staff looked perplexed. "But Mike," one of them asked, "can you give an example of a systems error that was thought to be a person's fault?"

"Sure," I responded. "Not long ago we had an all-nighter for our Middle School Ministry. Two buses went to a bowling alley with nearly one hundred young people. Everything went very well until the return trip. On the way back from the bowling alley, one of the buses broke down. As they pulled off to the side of the freeway, the kids were, understandably, upset—especially one young woman who had to catch an early flight to go on a cruise with her grandparents. While her mother waited in the church parking lot, her daughter was stranded in a broken-down bus—and getting very upset at the prospect of not getting to the airport on time. One of our policies establishes that a teen ministry staff member must make the determination whether to call the parents of a young person or not. The reasons are obvious—if kids are at all anxious about the event or just want to bail, that's not good enough to call parents. And our lay advisors understand this reasoning. We want to work with young people, not just ditch them when they don't feel like participating. And none of the adult advisors had their cell phones with them.

"So," I continued, "no one called the mom. The mom didn't find out about all that happened until the bus finally arrived, very late, and her (now hysterical) daughter rushed to the car. She did make the plane and had a good time on the cruise. But, long after the event, the parents of that girl were upset and, naturally, blamed our teen ministry staff person for the problem.

"But was it his fault? I don't think so. The problem was a systems error. First, the policy about not calling parents was too rigid and needed revision to make certain that special circumstances could be appropriately acted upon. Second, that no adult advisors had cell phones—as a matter of policy—needed to be revised. And last, the phone numbers of parents, though on a consent form, were not with the kids on the bus, so the call to that mom couldn't have been made while she waited in the parking lot anyway. If these changes had been in place, the appropriate and safe care for the young people, on a bus at the side of a busy freeway, could have been maintained even as this young woman's special needs were addressed. Addressing the systems issues depersonalizes the situation so that learning and appropriate adjustments can be made. If we had just blamed the staff person in charge, the necessary systems corrections would not have been identified, let alone made."

# Unintended Consequences

This is exactly the problem in the first church fight in Acts 6. The problem is of unintended consequences. We read: "*Now during those days, when the disciples were increasing in number, the Hellenists complained against the Hebrews because their widows were being neglected in the daily distribution of food*" (Acts 6:1).

The first noteworthy point in this passage is that the church was growing. The expansion of the Christian church that occurred in Acts 2 has continued. Everyone seemed to be doing the right things! The growth of the church, however, outpaced the infrastructure. Because the Jerusalem church held everything in common (Acts 2:44), the care of widows was essential. The daily distribution of food to them was literally a matter of life or death. But as the church exploded in growth, the system for caring about the widows broke down. Unfortunately, it seems to have broken down along social lines. And please note that the first response was blaming: "*The Hellenists complained against the Hebrews*" (Acts 6:1).

I find it interesting that infrastructure failures in the church usually manifest in systems of care. As the church grows, the expectations of care remain from a period when smaller groups of people could be more easily cared for. Just as in Acts 6, it takes time for the need to surface as well as for the system to adjust to a new reality. There is nothing in this text that suggests that the Apostles or the community as a whole didn't care about the Hellenists' widows. On the contrary, we shall see that a solution is found that addresses an accepted need.

The shift from membership to discipleship brings with it transitions like this one. Wise leaders and followers will understand that charges of lack of care or mis-set priorities are usually indications that the system has broken down. It is difficult to take our hearts out of the equation, but it is essential. When we take the criticism personally our defensiveness will automatically focus on the blame—at the expense of systems adjustment.

If, in the case of our broken-down bus, we had not heard the concerns of the mother, we would have lacked compassion. If we only addressed the blame in terms of the staff member, then making the essential changes to prevent a future occurrence would not have been made. Our infrastructure, in terms of policies and procedures, had not kept up with a growing ministry. Justice required that we hear this family and make appropriate changes that showed them, and others, that we had taken their concerns seriously.

# Expect Conflict

Those who are moving from membership to discipleship will have to shift their expectations. Whereas most Christians assume that the function of Christian leadership is to avoid conflict, disciple-making ministries understand that conflict is unavoidable. More than that, if the conflict is addressed it can be a truly creative moment for learning. This is exactly what happens in Acts 6. We read:

> And the twelve called together the whole community of the disciples and said, "It is not right that we should neglect the word of God in order to wait on tables. Therefore, friends, select from among yourselves seven men [and we would gratefully say, 'seven people'!] of good standing, full of the Spirit and of wisdom, whom we may appoint to this task, while we, for our part, will devote ourselves to prayer and to serving the word." (Acts 6:2-4)

There were sixty-five innovative pastors from two denominations. The event was sponsored by an insurance company. We were leading a group of pastors who had proven their abilities for ministry through innovation and success. It was an incredible experience. Afterwards, my colleague, Anthony Harris, and I began to collate our learning. We learned that innovators, no matter where they were on the theological or social spectrum—left or right or in-between—felt marginalized. But the most stunning learning was that those innovators in ministry with the greatest commitment to see it through were those who had a clear sense of "Call." While others were willing, almost eager, to talk of their hopes for their cause outside of the Christian context, those with a clear sense of "Call" spoke only of serving the Savior and making a lasting difference within the context of "church." The difference was that those who had a clear sense that they had been called by God to their tasks dealt with conflict and disappointment more easily. They knew that, for the sake of God's kingdom in Jesus Christ, conflict was not only inevitable but also a sign that they were doing their work.

> Conflict can be a truly creative moment for learning.

## Saying No in order to Say Yes

The apostles in Acts 6 face the conflict squarely and say no. They make it clear that they take the conflict and its issues seriously, but they know their jobs. Theirs is the "Call" to prayer and the word. Because they know their role in the community, they can both address the issue with care and make it clear that the solution is beyond them.

How many of us have wanted to say no in the Christian church? The problem is that we lack the clarity of the apostles that is necessary to say, with compassion and care, "This is not my job." The essential learning in this text is that we say no in order to say yes to what is ultimately more important. The apostles did not deny the problem. That is clear when they suggest a solution for it. But their acceptance of the seriousness of the issue at hand did not distract them from the job that God had called them to do.

That's what we discovered at the Innovations Conference that we lead. Those who faced and overcame conflict did so with a clear sense of their calling. This calling clarified the response that each of them felt compelled to make in response to very real and pressing issues or problems.

## Call clarifies response.

What is your calling? Every Christian is an eternal investment of God in this world. That means that God has created each person with a unique set of gifts, passions, and interests. God intends that this unique combination, refined by experience and training, will be set loose to bring the healing that only the reign of Christ can bring. The problem is that many of us settle for so much less. In the name of responding to the most pressing need, we set aside the special contribution that each of us can make toward a better world.

The Twelve would have none of that. They knew their unique calling: to serve the word and be in prayer. Because of this they could be open to a new day.

I looked out on the congregation. It was the second service at Our Savior's Lutheran Church in Salem, Oregon. I had noticed at the first service the attendance of a number of people I had never met. Simultaneously, I realized that I had seen them a lot. Then, at the second service, I looked out upon the very same phenomenon: the faces of individuals and families whose names I didn't know.

We were being blessed with growth. We had grown from an average attendance of about 120 to over 350—and now we were obviously growing again. I had visited every home of our new members and could call each one by name when I served them the Lord's Supper. Now, I could only recognize our regular visitors by face—no name came to mind.

I thought about it. After worship, I commented on what I had seen to my associate pastor and said, "I'm sure glad that you're visiting those folks and bringing them in." He looked at me and said, "Mike, I don't know if I've ever seen them before. I know I've never been in their homes."

How could this happen, I wondered. Our church had grown through a predictable process of visiting for worship, followed by a pastoral call, and then, frequently, the decision to join. Now what was I going to do if people were willing to visit us and, I later learned, contribute significantly without one of the pastors visiting them?

Was it right to grow this big? Was this a healthy way to grow? I remember praying about it in my daily devotions. I was struggling spiritually and pastorally. How could this happen, and how could we provide these newcomers with the services and ministry that we believed was needed?

Then it happened. One night as I prayed I remember hearing that inner voice that can only be the Holy Spirit. Usually I recognize the Spirit's counsel because it is a word that I couldn't have given myself, or it calls me to actions I am resisting mightily. That night the inner voice simply asked, "Mike, what right to do you have to limit the number of those I choose to bring into my church?" That night changed my life.

Since that time I have come to regard change as one of God's favorite teachers. If we are open to change, for the sake of Christ's mission, God will teach us wonderful and new lessons for effective ministry. The world changes, and our approach to the world will have to adapt to many of those changes. If you and I can welcome change as a spiritual teacher, then our hearts will be willing to follow the Spirit's leading.

> Regard change as one of God's favorite teachers.

I had to let go of a number of things in response to the Spirit's leading. I would need to see the local congregation differently. I would have to be open to God's invitation list that may or may not include those I had visited—or ever would visit. I began to open myself to the invitational ministry of our members and trust God to work in and through them.

And I began to relax. Like the Twelve in our text, I knew my job. My job was to lead our congregation by preaching the word and organizing teams. My job wasn't to manage for God how the church would grow. When you know who you are and what you're called to be about, ministry gets much easier. I was beginning to see members as disciples, even though I didn't know it. I was beginning to understand that the ministry of Christ's church is healthy when it is shared by all of God's people. My job was to learn how to grow deep as the congregation grew. Later I would discover how to be more intentional about the spiritual growth of disciples. That lesson would be learned at Prince of Peace.

# Soulful Self

Disciples emerge from members when individuals discover their unique contribution to the kingdom of God in the world. This discovery is the blessing of the Holy Spirit. I call it the "soulful self." Leading members into discipleship includes a process for this self-discovery. At Prince of Peace we use *Life Keys* as our tool to aid this wonderful awareness. *Life Keys* provides a comprehensive assessment that includes personality inventory, passions, and spiritual gifts. When disciples learn how God has gifted them, their sense of "Call" emerges. As they live out this call of God, their inner sense of purpose and accomplishment grows. Soulful self is the sense that "I have a unique gift to bring before Christ and to set loose for his purposes." All individuals or congregations who seek to discern how the Holy Spirit might best use them and how that can unleash their own significance will need to participate in an assessment tool that will unlock their soulful selves.

Soulful self is also the recognition that "my unique gifts are not less than any others." The confusion that our world imposes upon us is the blurring of role and value. We live in a world that is upside-down from the values of the kingdom of God. In the world our roles determine our values. Those whose roles are more public or bring greater power over others are assumed to have greater value than those whose roles in life do not. But Jesus teaches us that *"the greatest shall be least"*—his way of saying that role has little or nothing to do with eternal value. When we discover our soulful selves we discover that our value is determined by God, and our roles in life are simply expressions of our uniqueness interacting with circumstances. Christians must realize that role and value are separate.

A careful reading of Acts 6 will make it clear that the apostles did not think that their value was greater than those who would be called to be deacons in the first-century church. The *role* of the apostles was not to "wait on tables" but to advance the word and be in a healthy spiritual relationship with God.

How do you distinguish between role and value in your spiritual walk? Do you assume that the more public role brings greater value?

As you reflect on the above questions, ask yourself who the greatest spiritual influences have been in your life. Most of us will discover that those who brought the Lord Jesus nearest to us were rarely the objects of public acclaim. That doesn't mean that God cannot and does not use very public persons to support and bless our spiritual lives. But these figures often simply reinforce what we have experienced and learned from those closer to us.

"There are no jobs at Prince of Peace," I said. Looking at the staff, including custodians and secretaries and our media folk, I could tell that they were both most intrigued and most perplexed by that statement. "The truth is," I continued, "our custodians will be just as likely to be asked about spiritual health or what Prince of Peace really believes as will a pastor. The world has changed. With more people coming to our congregation from non-churched or de-churched backgrounds, their assumptions are that anyone who works at Prince of Peace is a spiritual guide. So, there are no jobs here—just the calling of God that will, hopefully, match your gifts and passions with a particular set of tasks. But if you don't see your work as the venue for your faith and witness, then you simply don't understand how God would use your unique talents for the sake of Christ's reign."

> The qualifications for ministry begin with spiritual integrity.

And they got it! The qualifications for ministry begin with spiritual integrity. Then a particular set of skills and work is added or developed.

The first-century Christian leaders understood this truth. So, they could celebrate their own inadequacies. They knew that they didn't know everything—and they didn't need to know everything! And that's when they invited the community of faith into the solution of the problem before them. *"Therefore, friends, select from among yourselves"* (Acts 6:3).

The Twelve didn't pretend to know the right people for the necessary task! Yet, how many of us in the twenty-first-century church feel the need to know everything? When we try to know all that is necessary we discourage others from participating in the work of the Holy Spirit to meet needs and solve problems. If the Twelve had thought that they needed to know who best could solve the problem at hand, one wonders how effective their selections would have been. Instead, the Twelve got out of the way and let the people find the solution.

Disciples are free from unreasonable expectations. We understand that one of the reasons our Savior created the church is that we cannot know all there is to know by ourselves. Yet, many leaders suffer from the anxiety and burnout of such an expectation. The consequence is that we feel the pressure of solving every problem ourselves—and the community is left out or its role diminished. When we are free from such delusional spirituality, we can live and help create a much healthier community where the gifts of each person can be celebrated.

The point is that the Twelve said no in order to say yes to the wisdom of the community. They didn't abrogate their roles. They didn't succumb to public opinion. Nor did they serve the god of ego in asserting their ultimate wisdom in the matter. In the gracious space between these two positions, they invited the community into a responsible role for meeting the need. The Twelve were willing to admit their limitations and trust the Holy Spirit at work within the community of disciples.

# Gifts-based Ministry

By articulating that everyone on staff has a call to ministry, I was uplifting a gifts-based ministry. Gifts-based ministries recognize that all are valued eternally by God, yet not all are equally gifted. The community of faith brings together a heaven-sent combination of personalities and gifts to serve the greater good. Where one is weak, another is strong. Where one role ends, another role begins.

Acts 6 is the birth of gifts-based ministry in the Christian church. The job description was clear: see to the daily distribution of food to the widows in such a manner that it is fair and sufficient to meet the needs. The criteria were also clear: persons known to the community for their personal integrity, empowered by the Holy Spirit for faith and service, and having a wisdom that is demonstrated through interpersonal relationships.

I have been guilty of the Membership Model for recruitment in ministry. In the Membership Model, the first, and often only, question is: Are they breathing? The tragedy of this method of recruiting for the work of God through the church is that it diminishes both the person and the purpose to which we call people. If the only criterion is an alive person who is simply willing to say yes, then anyone can do it. There is no celebration of gifts—nor is there, therefore, a clear call to serve. If these criteria dictate our selection process, then the work of the kingdom of God is denigrated to the level of menial tasks.

Disciples want to know that they have unique gifts to bring to the specific work at hand. More than that, they need to see the connections between God's purposes and the work to which they are being called. This is not the case in Acts 6. The specific ministry of serving was valuable enough to the community that "just anybody" couldn't do it. Those whom God had gifted would be known by the community, and their qualifications were determined by the leaders who understood the value of the work at hand.

Discipleship ministries strive to make the connections between the work of the kingdom and any task within a person's scope. If a clear link to God's kingdom cannot be made, why do it? What we long for is "holy work." This isn't a particular type of work, though many believe that it is. Rather, it is the significance we bring to our work.

Those who wash the floors or clean the toilets are either doing menial tasks or the work of the kingdom. The difference is the perspective and purpose workers bring to the task. If those who wash the floors or clean the restrooms pray for those who will walk those floors or use those facilities, then this can be holy work. If those who set up chairs for a particular event understand the possible impact of that event in the lives of those who attend and take the time to bathe the room with their prayers as they work, then the task is so much more than merely room set-up.

How does that work? The truth is that our restrooms are significant points of evangelism. If the restrooms are not clean and inviting, visitors will be less likely to return for worship in our facilities. If those who set up rooms or wash floors do not believe that their prayers and the welcoming impact of such set-ups will have an evangelical power, why do the work? Let those who come fend for themselves! The solution to so much of the minimizing of our lives is not to rush through our tasks and get on to something more enjoyable. Rather, it is to imbue the work with spiritual significance and surround the work in prayer.

# The Biblical Telescoping of Time

I have always found it intriguing that the scripture mentions the passage of time so infrequently. An example of this is in the text before us. Is it reasonable to imagine that the Twelve heard of the problem only once and then acted? Can we imagine that the grumbling and blaming of the Hellenists occurred only once, and then the solution was found? Probably not. What we have is the "telescoping of time."

When an object is far off we look through a telescope or pair of binoculars, and it suddenly looms near. In the Bible, what often took a considerable amount of time is "telescoped" into a short period of time with one verse following upon another. The likely scenario is that the Twelve heard about the grumblings only after they reached a level and intensity that required their attention. And it is only reasonable to suspect that the Twelve worked through the problem only after much prayer and conversation. Then they went public.

Disciples understand that what appears to be an immediate solution in the Bible probably took real time. We, therefore, understand that the best solutions usually occur only after the problem has been talked about in the congregation for some time and has finally reached a level that requires addressing. Then, we understand the need for conversation and prayer as essential elements for healthy decision-making. I believe that is what happened in Acts 6. No wonder it led to a marvelous up-building of the entire community of faith.

When significant issues surface in ministry, disciples understand that often the best action is none at all. Instead, there is an acknowledgment of the problem, serious prayer over it, and then conversation to find the best solution—not just one that works. Discipleship congregations institutionalize this process of prayer. Bible reading and prayer precede significant conversation as the open door for the Holy Spirit to enter and lead the discussion to its best solution.

Yet, most of our churches are established on a business model. We create an agenda with the expectation that each item will be addressed and a solution found or decision made. The idea that our conversations would include the elements of a healthy spiritual life, that the Holy Spirit might be interested in our conversation and actually willing to lead us, is often lost or only paid lip service.

At Prince of Peace our church board meets once a month for 90 minutes. The first 15–20 minutes are spent in prayer and a senior pastor's Bible study that focuses on leadership. We have experienced the power of the Holy Spirit to lead us and equip us to better lead our ministry through this discipline. If we need more time, and we occasionally do, then we consciously acknowledge that and continue. Or, we will set another meeting to address the unresolved issues before us. Usually, however, the time proves sufficient because we are conscious of the leading of God. And our work takes on the perspective of eternity.

Not long ago, we were discussing the need for a planning retreat for our church board. As we looked at our calendars and tried to find a day and time that would work for each of the ten of us, one of our board members spoke up.

"I have to tell you that I am deeply disappointed in the members of this board," he began—and you could have heard a pin drop as he looked at each of us in turn. "We are serving at an epic time in the ministry of this congregation. This is God's work. Instead of trying to fit it into our schedules, we ought to be committed to working our schedules around this task."

I was stunned. After thirty years in ministry, a lay leader had articulated what we had all longed to believe. We are not just about the business of an organization or institution. We are about God's work. The consequence was that a day and time was established and unanimous attendance was committed.

It must have been like that in the Jerusalem congregation after the Twelve spoke. We read: *"What they said pleased the whole community, and they chose"* (Acts 6:5). The Spirit of God united the congregation in purpose, and they set seven men before the apostles for commissioning.

# Identifying—Equipping—Empowering

The process before us is a three-step unleashing of the people of God. The community identified the seven for the task before them based on the criteria the Twelve had set forth. This was not a popularity contest. This process has little or nothing to do with most of our congregational annual meetings and the election of our church councils. There is no indication that these who were chosen were the most popular or had a hidden agenda or constituency. Their purpose was clear: see to the very real needs of the Hellenists' widows.

The equipping of these seven men had already occurred. That is how they were known to the congregation. What was left was for the leaders to publicly acknowledge their gifts, the specific calling of the task at hand, and then to empower them to serve. This happened with the laying on of hands and prayer.

All disciples are gifted, but not all are equipped and empowered for ministry. Discipleship ministries strive to embed the threefold process of Acts 6 in the fabric of the congregation. People are identified by gifts and passions. Then they are acknowledged, and specific skills or processes are taught them. Then they are turned loose for the ministry of the church by the leadership. As the congregation grows, the leaders will have to identify, equip, and empower more and more secondary leaders to accomplish this process.

**All disciples are gifted, but not all are equipped and empowered for ministry.**

For example, we have more than 120 lay ministers at Prince of Peace. These are those who have been identified with the spiritual gifts for this critical service. They are our front line in hospital calls, in support to the long-term ill or dying, and in support for those struggling with addictions. Yet, I know very few of them. Instead, one of our pastors works with a gifted lay minister on staff to identify, train, and commission these deacons of care for ministry in our congregation. As the personal circumstances of our lay ministers change, God provides others for this service. But our equipping makes it possible to confidently and publicly celebrate their gifts and service.

What would such a ministry look like in your congregation or your life? Wouldn't it look a lot like Acts 6?

When he first called for spiritual care for his wife who was struggling with breast cancer, he asked for a pastor. In fact, he insisted upon it. But as her disease continued, our pastor recommended a lay minister. "I am to be gone for the next two weeks, and I don't want your wife to be without care. As soon as I return," she said, "I'll check in with her and you." They grudgingly accepted the lay minister's visits.

Over the next year or more, the lay minister visited weekly and the pastor came occasionally. Finally, the earthly journey of this woman of faith was nearing its end. Once again, the husband called the church office. When he shared with our receptionist that his wife was in the last stages of dying, she quite naturally asked if he wanted a pastor to come over. There was a pause on the line, and then, he gently asked instead for the lay minister.

That's when it works! It's not about us and our need to be needed. It's about the gifts of God in the people of God turned loose for the kingdom of God!

We have had other experiences like this—as well as some not-so-pleasant ones. Not long ago we received a complaint that one of our lay ministers was abrupt and dogmatic in visiting disciple-members in the hospital. Our key staff asked the lay minister to come in and confronted him with the complaint. After a lengthy conversation, he asked if he could return to the hospital and apologize. After that experience his demeanor and ability to provide care improved dramatically. If it hadn't, we would have looked for another area for his service that would better fit his gift set. There are no failures in ministry—just misfits between

> There are no failures in ministry—just misfits between the gifts of the person and the particular work of the kingdom.

the gifts of the person and the particular work of the kingdom. So, we look for a better fit—and everybody wins.

# God's Progression

The outcome of such a gifts-based ministry is renewed energy and growth in the congregation. We read: "*The word of God continued to spread; the number of the disciples increased greatly in Jerusalem, and a great many of the priests became obedient to the faith*" (Acts 6:7).

Please note the progression in the text. From problem to gift-based ministry, the community of faith reached new depths in God. The outcome of this depth was growth through the spread of God's word. Numerical growth is the outcome of spiritual depth. We grow deep when we understand the connection of our gifts with the ministry of Christ's church. That's discipleship, not membership.

In God's divine progression, problems, conflicts, and frustrations are invitations to growth. What is necessary in order to experience that growth is to listen to the complaining (blaming) and hear the request within it. In every complaint is the expression of a need. When we hear the need we can better determine if the leader or the congregation can meet that need. There are some expressed needs that are in conflict with the identity, mission, and values of our particular ministry. That doesn't mean that the need is invalid. It means, rather, that our particular ministry cannot be the place to meet those needs.

In Acts 6, the Twelve determined that the need was legitimate. They then determined, as we have seen, that the best way to meet the need was to give it back to the disciples of the congregation with a proposed solution. This led to gifted persons becoming identified and commissioned for that need-meeting ministry. At the core of God's progression is our willingness to hear the need, decide where and how it is best met, and then implement a gifts-based response.

# From Doing to Equipping

In our time, gifts-based ministries are rarely established because our pastors have been trained in a credentialed world. By this I mean to say that the expectation of pastors by our congregations is for the pastor to be the "family chaplain." As a consequence, when complaints occur the assumption is that the pastor is responsible to make those upset, happy. Few clergy and lay leaders are comfortable with the process at work in Acts 6. Complaints are heard as legitimate needs that ought to automatically be taken seriously and alleviated. The cost to the mission of the church is enormous.

The first cost is to the focus of our ministries. If every need must be met, then the congregation has no unique identity, nor does it have a clear focus for its mission. Every complaint, no matter how petty or irresponsible, sets the agenda of the church.

Second, the loss of productive energy is tragic. Instead of harnessing the gifts of the people of God to advance the mission of the congregation, we spend time and effort on simply calming the waters. There are times when this is absolutely necessary, to be sure. But most of us in twenty-first-century ministry spend considerable time keeping things calm at the expense of forward movement. The Twelve affirmed the need but, after defining their roles and inviting the congregation of disciples into a new role for them, commissioned the gifted and advanced the mission of the Jerusalem church. The outcome was continued growth.

This provides a pattern for creating equipping ministries. The pastor must confront his or her own need to be needed. The deep need within every human being is for God. The pastor's role is to facilitate the individual, family, and community in a living relationship with the Holy Spirit. That means that pastoral work will be a part of what we do. But all Christians are called to pastoral work! The dumping of pastoral care onto the ordained fits the model of the pastor as professional with skills and gifts that no one else can aspire to. That time has passed. What the pastor does bring is an advanced knowledge of God's word, a practicing spiritual life, and the ability to apply these to his or her particular context. The role of the clergy in an equipping ministry is great indeed.

Notice, however, the critical shift in the behavior of the Twelve. They moved from "doing" to "equipping." Equipping ministries begin with the pastor choosing to become an equipper for all the people of God. In this model, strive to connect individuals with their gifts and then opportunities to use those gifts—as we have discussed above. These opportunities are not limited to ministry within the congregation. Some may be gifted as community leaders. An equipping church will help them identify their community service as a Christian ministry. Others will discover gifts for teaching, serving, leading, and pastoral care. The equipping church will help these gifted people of God find opportunities for effective use of those gifts within and beyond the congregation.

This movement to equipping leaders will require a decision on the part of the congregation that will affirm the personal shift within the pastor. The choice must be faced by the leaders and then disciples of a congregation in deciding whether they will both free the pastor from the Membership Model of expectations and welcome the gifted service of one another.

# Bridging the Gaps

One model for bridging the gap between the "membership expectations" of a congregation and the "gifted discipleship expectations" is how we introduce the ministry of gifted volunteers.

A few years ago, we discovered that if a pastor is willing to invest the time to equip spiritual caregivers, and then gradually introduce them into their ministry, an effective bridge could be built between what used to be and what is coming. Pastors can take lay ministers with them on house calls or hospital calls. Then, in their introduction of the caregiver, articulate that this person has been gifted and called by God to this ministry and, for the sake of maintaining a high level of care, will be visiting between the visits of the pastor. Next, the pastor equips the lay ministry with devotions and prayers. The lay minister then makes the visits. The pastor debriefs with the caregiver as well as with those who have been visited. Adjustments, improvements, and greater ease of service will result from these debriefings. There will be times when there isn't a good match between the lay visitor and the person being seen. Then the pastor can reenter the situation and, at an appropriate time, introduce another lay visitor.

While this calling, equipping, and commissioning is happening, the pastor will need to affirm the biblical and spiritual foundation for such a ministry. This happens by preaching and teaching the biblical call to gifts-based ministry. First Corinthians 12, Romans 12, and Acts 6 are only three of the many texts that affirm this model for discipleship congregations. Enlisting the support and providing the right language to our leadership ought to precede or coincide with the efforts to introduce gifted lay ministers or other aspects of gifts-based ministry.

The payoffs are wonderful. First, the pastor and leadership of the congregation will no longer carry the burden for the ministry by themselves. A team of active disciple-servants will emerge, first in one area and then in others. Second, those who have been called to ministries that fit their gifts and passions will experience an inner joy and sense of purpose that we all long for. They will, in fact, give us more of their own resources, time, and energy than we could have imagined. And they will open the congregation to more opportunities for serving and gifted engagement.

In every area in which we initiate gifts-based ministry, we are inviting our disciples to experience deep and sustained spiritual growth—which will grow the church of Jesus Christ. Stephen and Philip are examples of the invitation to continued growth through gifts-based ministry. Both grew beyond "waiting on tables." Because of their willingness to diligently serve they were equipped and called to greater service and leadership. Stephen became an incredible preacher and the first martyr of the Christian church. Philip becomes, as we will see, the model for the unleashing of God's people in witness by word and deed. When a gifts-based ministry is strategically implemented, the people of God grow. That's when the church grows.

# Ministry Teams

She came running up to me in the hallway of the seminary. I had been invited to speak to pastors and students about disciple-making ministry. "Mike," she said, "do you have just a moment?" And when I replied that I did, she said, "Wait here, I have to get my colleague."

In a moment she returned with her colleague and senior pastor. She said, "We just had to tell you that we heard you last summer and returned to our inner-city parish. We looked at the list of our volunteers and found we only had twenty-five active, regular volunteers in our congregation. So, we met with our council, and we all agreed to blow up our committees and move to ministry teams. We wanted to implement a gifts-based ministry."

"We did it all last September," her colleague continued. "So, what happened? Well, this January, only four months later, we have a volunteer list of over 125 persons. All because we turned them loose to serve where their hearts led them to serve. And we've never had so much fun!"

A ministry team is not a renamed committee. Committees were highly successful tools for achieving goals in the post–World War II era. As society developed and grew institutions, that institutional model was adopted by most of our congregations. The problem is that the generations that followed experienced committees as dead ends.

> **A ministry team is not a renamed committee.**

The definition of a committee in the words of an active twenty-eight-year-old woman I met in Baltimore, Maryland, is this: "A committee is a group of people who come together, talk a lot, and get nothing done."

Ministry teams exist to get things done. Their agendas serve the identified strategic steps necessary to accomplishing an agreed-upon task. Ministry teams meet only as necessary and only as long as it takes to get the job done. Committees, as most of us in the church know, take on a life of their own. They meet even when there is little or no need to meet and take up the time people assume a committee meeting ought to take. So, committees focus on themselves, their importance and power, not the mission of the church. Ministry teams can convene, plan, and then execute the plan. Then they will evaluate the plan and adjourn. They will reform only when another need arises.

Committees in our churches also abuse the time of our people. Most committees are controlled by the expectation that they cannot do anything until their plans have been approved by the church council. So, a person gives his or her time and energy only to have another group of people re-think their work in order to approve or disapprove of their actions. How tragic! The time of both the committee member and the member of the church council has been squandered. No wonder our churches meander without clear missional objectives—they are simply too busy checking up on each other!

Gifts-based ministries will be energy-producing ministries—not energy-consuming ones. And that's the model and outcome we discover in Acts 6.

# The Accountability Continuum

"But, Pastor Mike, where are the boundaries? This sounds like chaos to me," he said. I smiled and said, "That's where accountability comes in. Your concern is valid. But moving into a gifts-based ministry does mean a very limited exercise of control. Control is used in disciple-making ministries for only three reasons. The first is to pronounce dead a ministry that is already dead and gone."

The room erupted in laughter. We all know that in most of our churches the only thing harder than starting a new ministry is to kill one that is already dead. Discipleship leaders recognize the enormous amount of wasted energy—often accompanied by blame—that is spent on trying to revive a ministry no one wants anymore. At least we ought to control our ministries by caring enough for our people so that we pronounce dead what is revered for the sake of what once was and no longer has anything to do with what is or will be.

"The second reason for the exercise of executive control by the leaders is when a ministry that is critical to the mission of the church and valued by the congregation is being led ineffectively," I continued. "And I know of only one way to accomplish this. We have to be willing to 'fire' volunteers."

There were a few heads shaking and others nodding. So, I pressed my case.

"I remember when we decided to remodel our worship center. The board voted unanimously to do it. But we had hoped to receive all the pledges necessary to accomplish our task ahead of time so the board decided to build only what we could fund. The amount necessary was not pledged. The board," I continued, "was faced with the hard question of whether we would go ahead, contrary to what we had previously promised, or not. And if we did, who would announce the decision to the congregation. So, after lengthy debate and conversation the board decided to go ahead with the remodel and the board member who announced our previous commitment would have to stand before the congregation and explain why we were making a course correction."

I could see that the group was still with me so I continued my story: "We began the remodel and during our worship times invited groups to tour the space as it evolved. But on one occasion, a member of the board was walking with the tour and, all the while our staff leader was explaining our progress and the different direction of our worship space, the board member was loudly denouncing the decision and our action. But she had been a part of the decision making and had, in fact, voted to move ahead.

"That Monday morning I met with our staff leader, at his request, and, having heard his story, said we had to ask her to resign. He smiled and said, 'Thank you, I've already set an appointment with her.'

"Later that day, they met and the staff leader asked for the board member's resignation based on the public betrayal of the rest of the board and her unfair characterization of the decision-making process. The board member broke down and wept. Then she acknowledged that this was the right decision. And that's when it happened. She shared that her family was in real trouble and that all of her emotions just came out. She apologized. This volunteer was fired—and the system was self-correcting for health.

"If we hadn't held her accountable we would never have known her family situation. As it was, we were able to provide pastoral care and support at a critical time in her life. And she and her family continued to worship with us. Accountability isn't real if we are not willing to shift into control when necessary," I concluded.

"The third time control ought to be exercised is when a ministry is clearly violating the beliefs, values, or mission of the congregation. Such a ministry must be stopped, preferably before it starts," I explained.

A hand shot up, and, when acknowledged, the woman said, "But Mike, you're suggesting that accountability is not the opposite of control, and I always thought it was."

"The truth of the matter is that *abdication* is the opposite of control," I said. "I have developed an accountability continuum with the opposite poles being control and abdication, and accountability is in the center. There are times when control will have to be exercised, as I have explained. There are also times when we can abdicate direct involvement in a ministry. When a lay leader, for example, has demonstrated consistency in effective, missional ministry we can let them go. I would suggest that we bless their ministry and offer to be present whenever they need us, but otherwise they are on their own. That's abdication."

"Accountability is the coaching presence of a leader. We equip by providing the necessary skill base, making clear to whom the volunteer is responsible and for what. Then we provide regular times for checking in. We might drop in on their ministry to thank them or observe how things are going. If necessary we can intervene. But the lines of accountability are clear. In accountability systems individuals and groups have a great deal of freedom with support. But whatever they do, the role of the leader is to make the connections of their efforts to the disciple-making ministry of the congregation clear. Most of us want to see how our efforts advance a much larger vision of Christ's church in mission."

# Questions and Reflections

Gather with other disciples and ask the following questions:

1. How much of the energy in our congregation is lost in blaming? How might we discipline ourselves to always ask the systems question first?

2. Are we willing to anticipate conflict as a predictable outcome of succeeding in our mission? How could we help to form a congregation where conflict is understood as a learning moment?

3. Is your understanding of the size of the "proper" congregation limiting what the Holy Spirit would accomplish in and through your congregation? Can the growth of your congregation be stifled by your understanding of "how" God grows a church? Are you open to the counsel of the Holy Spirit? What would you need to give up in order to receive that counsel?

4. Is your ministry a gifts-based one? If not, what strategic steps will need to be implemented to move towards a gifts-based ministry? Where will the resistance come from, and how might you both anticipate it and lessen its impact in your congregation?

5. Do you believe that congregational leaders could and should fire volunteers? What processes would need to be established for a healthy recognition and promotion of volunteers as well as for a consistent and healthy firing?

6. On a scale of 1 to 5, what is the energy level in your congregation? One could mean very low, 2 would mean below average, 3 could mean at a maintenance level, 4 would mean building, and 5 would be exciting and missional levels of energy. If it is below 4, how might you bring energy to your ministry? If it is at a 4 or 5 level, what is happening, and how could you celebrate that and invite others into your growing ministry?

IV

# AN UNSTOPPABLE POWER—ACTS 8

The economic aftershocks of the planes crashing into the World Trade Towers and the Pentagon were enormous. In our area, anxiety was fueled by job loss as well as the threat of terrorism. The consequence was that churches were facing a shortage of funds, along with most other institutions and businesses.

In the midst of this economic crisis, I received a visit from two of our disciples at Prince of Peace. As we chatted, I discovered that they had been meeting with another lay leader and exploring the possibility of a ministry to those who had lost jobs. More specifically, they didn't want another grief or support group. They wanted a ministry where that would be present, but the focus would be on connecting those seeking work with employers who had jobs to offer. They had visited a number of sites where such ministries were being offered and had a design they wanted to implement in our community on behalf of Prince of Peace. I shared their enthusiasm for this new mission effort. But I couldn't help asking why they wanted to meet with me.

"Well," one of them responded, "we wanted your approval."

"OK," I replied. "Let me ask you two questions. Does this fit as part of your personal discipleship? And, if so, does it strive to meet a real need in keeping with our vision and the Marks of Discipleship?"

They both nodded. "In fact," the other leader said, "this is how I want to serve within and beyond Prince of Peace. And I know there is a great need for help. I've been without a job, and I know how important a ministry like this could be. And, since we've learned from other models, I think this will be successful."

"You don't need my approval," I said. "What you can count on is my support, and if I can be helpful, just let me know. But in our system, if you can align a ministry with our disciple-making ministry and meet a real need, just go for it!"

I then told them the staff person to whom they ought to report. Then we prayed together.

From the crisis in our community and church, three disciples launched a significant ministry. Literally hundreds of individuals have been supported and helped through this ministry. The vast majority of them are not affiliated with Prince of Peace. Over and over again in multiple conversations in the upper Midwest, I have had people share stories with me about how our "Job Connections" ministry helped them or someone they knew. One such conversation occurred while I was serving jury duty for our county in a community about thirty miles away from Burnsville. One of my fellow jurors told me that he knew Prince of Peace because when he was out of work he attended our Jobs Connections group. He shared how helpful and supportive it was!

# The End as the Beginning

In Acts 8, the question is how the Christian church will respond to crisis. The response of the Jerusalem congregation to both the martyrdom of Stephen and the subsequent persecution is remarkable. These first-century Christians would discover the faithfulness of God and turn a crisis into a mission opportunity. We read:

> That day a severe persecution began against the church in Jerusalem, and all except the apostles were scattered throughout the countryside of Judea and Samaria. Devout men buried Stephen and made loud lamentation over him. But Saul was ravaging the church by entering house after house; dragging off both men and women, he committed them to prison. **Now those who were scattered went from place to place, proclaiming the word.** (Acts 8:1-4, emphasis added)

The end was the beginning for these Christians. In fact, this crisis would be the catalyst for their fulfilling the command of Jesus. In Acts 1:8 we read: *"But you will receive power when the Holy Spirit has come upon you; and you will be my witnesses in Jerusalem, in all Judea and Samaria, and to the ends of the earth."* But the Christian church, according to Luke, stayed in

Jerusalem until the martyrdom of Stephen; the following persecution pro-
pelled them out into the surrounding area. This expulsion, and the pursuit of Saul (Paul) will be the launching pad for going into mission into
the world. Prior to the events in Acts 8, to be a Christian was to come to
Jerusalem—not go from Jerusalem into the world!

That's what three disciples of Prince of Peace did. They began to see
the very real ministry opportunity God was setting before us through an
economic crisis. As one company after another activated cutbacks and
"right-sizing," the human cost was enormous. Rather than stand passively
by and simply "feel badly," these three leaders began exploring the alter-
natives already available and how they worked. Then, selecting some of
the best from among the models operating, and determining that there
was a very real need for a Job Connections ministry in our area, they came
for the senior pastor's blessing—and got it. Frankly, I was both humbled
and proud of their passion and diligence.

# A People Empowered

In Acts 8 the text is quite clear about how the crisis became a missional
opportunity. The apostles stayed in Jerusalem. That means that those
"devout men" who buried Stephen were the apostles. The people were
scattered. The people became the missionaries that "proclaimed the
word" in the places they fled to.

Between Acts 6 and Acts 8 a remarkable effort had obviously been
orchestrated by the Holy Spirit. The
apostles were modeling and equipping
the people for witness in word and deed.
The critical shift here is not in the content of the word. Instead it occurs in the
*carriers* of the word. From the apostles to
the people, the word of God was liber-
ated from a few leaders to the whole
church.

> The critical shift occurs in the *carriers* of the word.

"You are the missionaries of the twenty-first century," I said. I was
preaching on Acts 2 and the empowering of the Holy Spirit. I had shared
that the Spirit clearly descended on all who had gathered together, not
just the twelve apostles. All had become witnesses. But I also traced how
we in the western world had taken the witness of all God's people, and,

by institutionalizing our churches and through the training of our pastors, relegated it to the activity of a few. It was a counter-Pentecost! The evangelists were thought to be the pastors. The evangelism of the laity was to support pastors who did it.

But the world has shifted again. What once seemed to advance the growth of God's church now is its hindrance. In a time and society where distrust of leadership is so prevalent, and skepticism meets the witness to our faith, a new missionary is called forth. The people of God are our missionaries. Our neighbors and friends outside the Christian church will be persuaded, not by clarity of doctrine or the preaching of the pastor, but through living discipleship. When they see adults, young people, and children striving to live their faith and open to discussing what they believe and why, the mission of the gospel is advanced.

"You are the missionaries of the twenty-first century," I said. "You will be invited into places and conversations that I as a pastor will never go. If you are willing to take your faith with you and simply be open, God will present possibilities for witness that you cannot imagine. And all God asks for is a willingness—not perfection. In the authentic witness of real people in real-life situations, the Holy Spirit will change the world in the name of Jesus Christ."

That's what happened in Acts 8. This is an old and a new vision for the church. The Reformation principle of the priesthood of all believers is being resurrected in our time as more than just a theological concept. In the past, I have—along with countless other well-meaning pastors—paid lip service to this great calling of God to the entire people of God. Even as I preached on the priesthood of all believers, I behaved as if I were the only real witness in the church. And the congregation was delighted to let me do it!

# De-credential Your Church

How do we embrace the unstoppable power of God's people in mission? First, we must de-credential our ministries. As long as only the ordained or officially licensed can truly witness to the gospel, we will be stuck in Jerusalem. As long as we are limited by a spiritual elite who have been credentialed by the church, the unstoppable force that is the priesthood of all believers will be just one more good idea.

I am not suggesting that we do not have ordained or trained clergy. I am suggesting that the content of that training has to change in order to achieve a new outcome for our new era. Those ministries where the pastoral leaders join with lay leaders to empower the whole church for *actual ministry in real life* will grow deep and wide. Those ministries that continue to see the pastor as the hired evangelist and spiritual elite, will continue to decline. They are stuck in Jerusalem.

De-credentialing our ministries begins when the ordained see their training as equipping them to be equippers of the missionaries of our time: our disciples. Discipleship always and necessarily leads to apostolic witness. That witness will not happen until our disciples understand themselves as the embodiment of the Christian

> **Discipleship always and necessarily leads to apostolic witness.**

church wherever they are and with whomever they are.

Second then, we need to redefine our ministries and ministers. As long as the disciples at Prince of Peace see the senior pastor and our other pastors as the real ministers, then the innovative and passionate efforts of people like those who created and have sustained our Job Connections ministry will never happen. As long as our committees and their chairs understand their jobs to be the only authenticators of good ministries, we will be stuck in Jerusalem.

We cannot imagine that the apostles in Jerusalem maintained control of the activities of the scattered disciples. They prayed for them, to be sure. Probably, they would counsel when asked and from afar. But the Holy Spirit and the teaching of the apostles were the only boundaries for their witness.

I believe we need to discover such heavenly freedom in our churches. Pastors grow disciples deep in God's word. Then we equip disciples to understand that all of us have a calling from God to bear witness to the risen Savior, Jesus. The how of that, as well as the where and with whom of that, will be discovered as we are open to the leading of the Holy Spirit. We return to church to worship, recover, and be renewed so that we can reenter into the world God loves so much.

I was teaching a Bible class on Monday night. I looked out at those who were in attendance and saw Sharon. She wore a colorful scarf around her head because she was undergoing chemotherapy for cancer of the uterus. And she was alone because her husband, Dale, was home recovering from treatment for his leukemia.

After the lesson she approached me and hugged me. "Thank you so much for tonight's teaching, Pastor Mike," she said. "You can't imagine how good it is to be here."

"Sharon, I saw you here tonight and was so blessed that you came. How is Dale?"

"Well, would you please pray for him? I'm doing well, but he is really struggling," she replied. So, together we stopped, and, joining our hands, I prayed for her and her husband, Dale.

"Sharon," I said after the prayer, "I'd love to come over to the house and pray with you and Dale, anoint you both with oil and lay hands upon you both for healing. What night would work this week?"

"Any night but Wednesday, Pastor Mike," she replied. "On Wednesday the Prince of Peace prayer ministry team is coming to pray over us."

And I got it. I knew what I had just done and was bound and determined to get out of it. I had just slipped back into my caring heart and credentialed world.

"Oh, Sharon," I replied, "you don't need me to come over. God will surely hear the prayers of our prayer ministers just as quickly and deeply as mine. But I will be in prayer for you and Dale."

And Sharon, this wonderful woman of faith, smiled because she knew it was the truth.

A de-credentialed ministry lifts up the power of God in all of God's people. Every pastor I have ever spoken with acknowledges that there are people within our congregations that are more spiritually gifted than we are. Likewise, we often recognize how God has gifted some for pastoral care at a level that is nothing short of amazing. But in our credentialed world, only those with the "sheepskin" are publicly commissioned and expected to act. The consequence is that the churches are filled with gifted disciples who cannot and do not, for a variety of reasons, share their gifts. No wonder we are so frustrated. Instead of experiencing an unstoppable power, we are stuck. All of God's people will be missionaries when the credentialed understand that our training is intended to be a gift to bless, train, and turn loose all of God's people in the power of the Holy Spirit.

What would happen if our churches sought out our praying saints and invited them into a ministry for the congregation? Those called to prayer could uplift worship before or as it occurs. They could be present to anyone who desires prayers for any reason. They could visit the sick and shut-ins to provide spiritual care and support. When only the pastor does these things, we limit the gifts and power of the church. Good deeds lead to good thinking. Good words spring from good hearts. Good hearts grow when they practice their faith through trusting God in daring good deeds. It's not linear. It's circular. But if we do not call forth and bless the good deeds of every disciple—especially as they live out of their gifts—we should not be surprised when our ministries flag and God's people functionally separate their relationship with Jesus Christ from the rest of their lives.

# Philip's Example as Outcome

The witness of the New Testament is incarnational. This is true of Jesus. It is also true of the followers of Jesus. Whenever a disciple is empowered by the Holy Spirit, she or he incarnates the Christian church. Philip is the example in Acts 8. He provides for us the outcome that we are called to anticipate as we move to an empowered people of God. We read:

> Philip went down to the city of Samaria and proclaimed the Messiah to them. The crowds with one accord listened eagerly to what was said by Philip, hearing and seeing the signs that he did, for unclean spirits, crying with loud shrieks, came out of many who were possessed; and many others who were paralyzed or lame were cured. So there was great joy in that city. (Acts 8:5-8)

Philip is not the only one doing these great things. Acts 8:4 tell us that all the people who were scattered proclaimed the word. We can assume that Philip is simply a noted example of what all the people were doing. The outcome of the ministry of the Twelve in Jerusalem was the spiritual growth of Philip who, having faithfully served by waiting on the Hellenistic widows, now is called to become an evangelist. Philip is just one among the many who grew deep and then were called out into mission.

As an example, Philip reveals the integrity of witness that the Christian church is called to exhibit. This integrity comes when the word we preach is demonstrated in the work we do. The word we proclaim is of the Messiah, Jesus. The work we do is our serving in Jesus' name.

The twenty-first century is a suspicious time. In our society people are suspicious even of charity. When I have stopped to offer aid to stranded motorists, I have been most frequently met by suspicion and fear. When churches reach out to serve their communities they often have to make absolutely clear that their motivation comes from their hearts of faith. Otherwise, our efforts are easily discounted as motivated by "getting more people into the church." Such a motive is experienced by those outside of our congregations as self-serving and institutionally driven. Naming the name of Jesus frees the served to receive the servers with less suspicion. And the witness is incredible. The world takes notice.

> "It ought to be possible to live a Christian life without being a Christian," laments Roy Hattersly, a columnist for the *U.K. Guardian.* Hattersly, an outspoken atheist, came to this conclusion after watching the Salvation Army lead several other faith-based organizations in the relief effort after Hurricane Katrina. "Notable by their absence," he says, were "teams from rationalist societies, free thinkers' clubs, and atheists' associations—the sort of people who scoff at religion's intellectual absurdity." According to Hattersly, it is an unavoidable conclusion that Christians "are the people most likely to take the risks and make the sacrifices involved in helping others." (*Leadership,* vol. 27, no. 2: 67)

The witness of the Christian church has, from the beginning, been in word and deed. The naming of Christ is our claiming of the power of Christ. This is the source of our willingness to risk for the sake of others, whether the crisis to which we respond is ours or theirs. With Jesus at the center of our ministries, there is an integrity that cannot help but be noticed. That's what the atheist Roy Hattersly teaches us. We can be dismissed for many reasons. But when we combine our trust in Jesus Christ with a missional zeal to change the world through concrete acts of service and care, even our most ardent critics take notice.

Recently at Prince of Peace we have experienced the power of translating our words into deeds. When we were invited by the City of Burnsville into two low-income housing projects to provide support and presence, we went. That ministry eventually morphed into our Mission Outpost. Serving a greater variety and number of those in need, we have provided food and clothing for nearly 1,000 families over the past year. We have delivered over 5,000 pieces of furniture to those who could not afford to buy furniture for their apartments or homes. Last November we provided Thanksgiving meals for a family of eight that would be enough for two more meals. And at our Mission Outpost and with those Thanksgiving meals we provide New Testaments in English and in Spanish.

The result is that Prince of Peace is becoming known as a church that cares. When there was a series of deaths among young people in our area, our teen ministries staff members were present in the high schools. When a funeral was conducted, whether at Prince of Peace or elsewhere, they were visibly present to support and reach out. The consequence is that, though our community has been 99 percent developed, our children's and teen ministries have continued to grow and remain strong.

# Joy

Prince of Peace exists to bring joy to the lives of our disciples and to our community. We need to distinguish joy from "happy." We, as a society, have become addicted to happy. Happy is the inner feeling of elation that occurs because of an external stimulus. We experience happiness when things are going well or we are having fun. "Happy" is a response to what is happening to us. So, when we are unhappy or discontent, we buy something new, try on a new relationship, or look for fun.

The Bible speaks of joy as an inner peace and confidence that is experienced within a person regardless of external circumstances. It has been said that joy is the consequence of three critical elements in the lives of individuals. These three necessary elements are: (1) relationships that work; (2) work that matters to the individual; and (3) a purpose beyond the individual.

Relationships that work stand the test of time. These are the friendships and love relationships that travel through the ups and downs of our lives as a thread of hope and support. Relationships based on "happy" will not, indeed cannot, stand the test of time. In the Christian church we discuss relationships in terms of eternity—now that's a long time! Our desire is to live in such a relationship with Jesus Christ and to engage with others from that perspective. The Christian church stands in support of relationships that work. Not all relationships work. Where there is abuse the abuse must stop, or the victim has the right to leave that relationship. Where relationships are destructive or surrounded in pretense, the Christian church encourages appropriate health-giving action.

Work that matters is fundamentally soul work. If we cannot bring our souls to work, it cannot ultimately matter. When we work just for a paycheck, we do not engage in work that matters. But when our work can be connected to our faith, or as an activity for the greater good, then we discover significance in our labor. The Christian understanding of vocation—work as a God-given call—is the call to joy.

> **Work that matters is fundamentally soul work.**

When Christians discover, as those who fled Jerusalem did, that our lives serve the eternal kingdom of God, then we have a purpose that is beyond ourselves. Our lives are missional—not just our churches. That is the great discipleship lesson of Acts 8:8.

One of the most frequently repeated phrases in the Christian church comes from those who reach out in service to others. We hear again and again that they "received more than they could have possibly given." Though there is no quantitative measurement for this, those who say it are convinced it is true. Those who give the most frequently are those who have experienced this joy of service. No wonder they keep returning to serve in our ministries. The outcome of our work is not simply that the lives of others are blessed—as wonderful as that may be. We are blessed. We receive joy. When we invite others into the life of faith, we are inviting them to joy.

# An Evangelism of Joy

I have come to believe that when Jesus promised that he had come to give us *abundant life* he wasn't speaking of inheriting that abundance after we die. The abundant life is our foretaste of the life to come. When the members of our churches are transformed into disciples their lives change. The focus of their involvement and the function of the church radically turn outward. If positive psychologists are telling us the truth, such an outward focus is essential for joy because we begin to live for a purpose beyond ourselves. As long as we are focused on "what's in it for me," joy is not possible and we settle for the merely "happy." God calls us to so much more than that.

This then becomes the basis for our disciples' missionary activities. Instead of focusing on who is in or out of heaven, we can turn our attention to an invitation to joy in this life.

Not long ago I had a conversation with a disciple about this very issue. He and his wife had faced significant challenges in their lives together, culminating in her recent illness. But her courage and his support were upheld in the promise and purpose of their shared faith. At the end of the conversation, this highly successful lawyer looked at me and simply said, "I can't imagine what it would be like for people to go through these things without faith or without the church." That is the basis for an evangelism of joy—not judgment.

The outcome of joy for Philip, and one would assume the witness of the others who were scattered, was the result of a practical Christian engagement in the world. Two elements identified in our text leap out as essentials to that engagement. These two elements added to the power and authenticity of the witness to Jesus as Savior.

The first is liberation. Freedom from demonic possession can be understood as spiritual and emotional liberation. In our pre-Christian world, we are reassessing the reality of the demonic. As many pastors, theologians, and disciple-members in our churches do this reassessment there is a wonderful reclaiming of the power of the Holy Spirit to defeat evil in all of its forms. When the Berlin Wall fell many looked to the Christian churches as places of meeting for those who would stand against the demonic tyranny of the former Soviet Union. Liberation as an outcome of the servant church was visible. Similarly, the reconciliation process at work in South Africa is a direct outgrowth of applying the truth of the gospel to overcoming evil and its consequences. Still others among us have been involved in prayers to free individuals from demonic possession. All are exercises of liberation in the name of the great liberator, Jesus.

The second element is healing. As more of our disciple-members have experienced the empowering of God, through biblical grounding and the power of prayer, there has emerged a remarkable rebirth of healing ministries. Regardless of the mixed results of experiments in prayer, increasing numbers of our people as well as the population at large continue to look to the Christian community for prayers of healing. At Prince of Peace this has led to a lay ministry program that is increasing. More than that, more of our disciple-members are in prayer for others in their neighborhoods and in relationships of friendship and love.

# The Ministry of Prayer

I was out walking my dog when a neighbor and disciple-member at Prince of Peace called to me from her back door. I stopped, and she approached to tell me of the sudden medical problem of one of her friends, also at Prince of Peace. She then told me how, when she first got the word, she immediately called her fiancé at his place of work and said, "Dean, you've got to stop doing whatever it is you're doing and pray with me." And he did. And they prayed.

Imagine the power and witness of this experience. Here we have two people who are willing and committed to trust God with those they care about. More than that, they are willing to stop whatever they are doing and, no matter who may be watching in his case, pray for someone in need. That's a healing ministry that bears witness to the presence of faith. And, as we have seen, the world takes notice.

Leader-disciples who want to make the shift to disciple-making ministries will implement strategic prayer. Unless the Holy Spirit is present and active the mission of the Christian church is without power. But when we pray we dare to believe that the very power of God is set loose. We trust that unleashing of power because we cannot know nor predict what it will accomplish in and through us. But as we pray our hearts and eyes are opened and we discover the work of the Holy Spirit—which, of course, leads us into more prayer and an active, missional church.

Start by inviting those who believe in the power of prayer, as well as those who would be willing to grow in their practice of prayer, to come together on a regular basis. Establish the appropriate rules of confidentiality: what is prayed about in specific stays in the hearts of those who pray, no one should bring up the name of someone who hasn't given them permission to do so, and so forth. Then ask for a commitment to meet together for at least seven times and to keep a prayer list. The prayer list is for two reasons. The first is so that each pray-er can continue to pray individually for those things the group has joined in prayer about. The second is so that the answers to prayer can be celebrated and shared. Each time of prayer will include appropriate updates on those persons and issues for which the group has prayed as well as new prayer concerns.

It is important to exercise caution in soliciting and praying for the medical needs of others. This is necessary because of the confidential nature of those needs. Specific sharing, about the medical needs or condition of those for whom we pray, can be allowed only with the permission of the individual or, if he or she is incapacitated, the family. For some people, both within and outside of the church, these can be highly personal matters. The Christian ministry of prayer is not helped by intruding, unwanted, into the details of the lives of others.

But make one of your prayer concerns the mission of the congregation. As disciples pray for their church they will be asking for the Holy Spirit to empower the congregation for more effective mission and ministry. Prayers for the unity of the congregation are also essential. Many of us can testify to the truth that conflict is always a twin to growing effective ministry.

# A Refocused Church

He was broke. He had not only lost his business but also had to file for personal bankruptcy. I suspect that if you and I were disinterested observers we would have said it was all over. We would have thought it impossible for anyone to crawl out of a hole that deep.

But he did. It wasn't easy. It certainly wasn't by listening to those who said it couldn't be done. He and his wife simply started one step at a time, one day at a time. And he relocated and rebuilt his business. You could call it grit, or optimism, or a "never say die" spirit—and you'd certainly be right. But if you asked him and his wife, as I did, they'd tell you it was God—and faith. Their faith in Jesus Christ grounded them in the God who never gives up on anyone. This is the God who transforms death into new life. That's what they said. And, having said that, they will tell you that's why people should never give up on themselves.

The reader has probably figured out that my conviction is that the Christian church will only effectively meet the challenges of our time through a radical refocusing of the lens. Instead of focusing our efforts on the institution of the church, we ought to focus on the people in Christ's church. When we grow a faith in one another, like that couple had developed, living discipleship emerges. Living discipleship cannot help but worship, read God's word, pray, serve, relate to others spiritually and give of our substance. And the world notices this witness.

> When we grow a faith in one another, living discipleship emerges.

Discipleship dares to grow Christ's church by growing Christ's people. Then the Holy Spirit, as we have seen in Acts 8, will lead the people of God into the world to witness to the truth of the Messiah in word and deed.

I can't help but wonder if we had been in Jerusalem watching the events of Stephen's martyrdom and the vicious persecution of this fledgling movement that followed Jesus of Nazareth, would we have thought it was all over. Their leaders are under control because the religious powers know where they are and can track and control what they will do. And the followers have been cut off from these leaders and scattered. It must have looked like a done deal.

It wasn't. The focus of the message of the gospel became the living faith of all those who had come to experience the faithful presence of God. They knew that the One they worshiped had already conquered death. Giving up on themselves and God was simply not an option—just like my friends I mentioned earlier.

In our time, many have written the epitaph of the Protestant church in America. They have suggested that the institution is run-down, the leaders demoralized, and the followers scattered and no longer attending the church. If we focus on the loss of membership, the number of clergy who have left active ministry or have fallen due to moral failure, the number of grand old buildings that are vacant or nearly so, then they may be right. But if we focus on the faith of individuals and families, if we listen to the stories of those whose faith has seen them through incredibly difficult times, and if we then listen to the spiritual hunger of our time, I believe we have great cause for hope.

Besides, we worship the God of new beginnings . . . not dead ends.

# Questions and Reflections

1. How are you experiencing the power of prayer in your church? Do you have a group that regularly meets and prays for the congregation as well as for other needs? If not, will you make the effort to invite others to join you in such a ministry?

2. What is the most significant learning from this chapter for you?

3. Have you seen how a crisis can become an opportunity for ministry?

4. What would be necessary to "de-credential" your church?

5. Choose one concrete action that would move your congregation into being a people of witness.

6. Gather with a group of brother and sister disciples. Answer the question: What would our church look like if we all saw ourselves as missionaries? Perhaps you could draw illustrations of what that would look like. Pray over the dreams that come.

7. What would an evangelism of joy look like in your congregation?

8. How can you refocus the ministry of your congregation from budgets to people, from institutional needs to the spiritual needs of disciples? How would you know this refocusing had been accomplished? What would it look like?

V

# THE POWER OF VISION—ACTS 16:6-10

"Mike," she said, "you're too stuck down in the mire." Elaine is one of the executive team members of the church board at Prince of Peace. I had submitted an extensive set of key objectives based on the singular goal of growing deeper discipleship at Prince of Peace. Having had time to process them with the board as a whole and now with the executive team, Elaine was willing to push me. She wasn't alone. As the vice president of our board, she was joined by Lynette, our president—and the other members, Curt and Brian, agreed. "You need to think in terms of the whole environment of Prince of Peace," Elaine continued. "Maybe articulate three or four themes, and then keep the concrete objectives to one or two beneath each theme." She smiled then and said, "If possible, that is."

We all laughed. As we had prayed over the process for aligning the ministries of Prince of Peace, we had also prayed over the board involvement and my leadership. Instinctively, I knew that they were right. My job was to lead an entire ministry. I was to serve as a cultural co-creator with the Holy Spirit. Into that spiritual architecture I would invite key lay leaders, key staff leaders and then the whole church.

The following is the document prepared for and adopted by the church board.

Senior Pastor's Goal, Themes, and Objectives
2006

Having had significant conversation around the goal and objectives previously proposed, I have been encouraged to think at a "higher level." This seems right. So, here is the goal with five Key Themes for my work. Under each theme is at least one, but no more than three, critical objectives for the advancing of that Key Theme. This approach acknowledges that my work is fundamentally that of an architect—prayerfully working with God's Holy Spirit to renew and shape the culture of Prince of Peace.

Goal/Mission: To increase and deepen the living discipleship of those affiliated with Prince of Peace.

*Tag Line: Real Faith for Real Life*

Vision: Prince of Peace will be the center for equipping individuals, families, and ministries to engage in growing deeper in faith so that they will enter into our world and impact it with a witness of faith and compassion. Our disciples will be visibly involved in our ministries, supporting them through their consistent stewardship of time and finances, as well as helping to shape our evangelical ministry, serving a greater variety of persons from many ethnic or socio-economic groups.

*Tag Line: A Church for the World and the World in a Church*

Key Themes:

I.   Personal Spiritual Integrity
II.  Connections
III. Deeper Biblical Faith
IV.  Space
V.   Outreach

Objectives:

Personal Spiritual Integrity:
- Deepen my practice of the Marks of Discipleship

Connections:
- Create an environment of "Three Touches"
- Institutionalize continuous formation and reformation of small groups within Prince of Peace

Deeper Biblical Faith:
- Quarterly, topical, biblical teachings

Space:
- Develop and present building plans that address the needs of the congregation for present and future ministry

Outreach:
- Lift up, encourage, and affirm expanding the various expressions of our mission to new areas of need
- Reflect the diversity of our community and world in *how* and *what* we do to meet the needs of others in Jesus' name.

Later I e-mailed this explanation, goal, and vision to both Elaine and Lynette. Subsequently, it went before the board and our executive staff team. All agreed that it was at the right level for my work.

The next step in the alignment process was to secure from each of the executive staff team members their annual goals and objectives and make certain that they line up in support of these themes. These were taken to the board for their conversation. Subsequent to the board's conversation, they would be implemented.

As a part of the implementation process, each executive staff team member took the themes to their supervisees, and, sharing their own goals and objectives, aligned the staff members' programs or support activities to the overall themes articulated.

The point is that this process will, hopefully, help create two mundane miracles: focus and momentum.

# Focus

The problem with many of our ministries is that we lack focus. We believe that we should do all that we can, and that is good. The problem with that is that we deplete our resources on what is good, not what is best. God calls us to serve beyond the merely good. Each of us has been placed in a time and space for ministry. Since we do not believe in a capricious God, that means that there is a reason for the particularity of our ministries. Unfortunately, we rarely get to that particularity. Instead, we try to provide what our traditions require and, if the time allows, to serve whatever seems to be the most urgent need.

Focus, which is the challenge of the five themes for the next five years at Prince of Peace, is the leadership attempt to discover, define, and refine (over time) the particularity of our ministries. Without a clear focus, we are rarely able to assess our successes or failures. The mission of the church defines its focus. The vision anticipates its future. The themes or objectives clarify the leader's activities that help fulfill the goal and advance toward the vision. A "tag line" is the simple language to communicate a particular aspect of the ministry of a congregation. The tag line simply expresses, in our case, both the mission and vision. These provide the focus and require critical and strategic decisions to be made to advance toward the goal with clarity of purpose.

Focus helps us say no. In the absence of focus, we can assess our ministries only on the basis of the "soft" measurements of how we feel, how others seem to feel, or the general mood of the congregation. Or, we resort to the hard measurements of receipts, worship attendance, and so forth. Any, or all, of these measurements may tell us a part of the truth, but they provide a false sense of reality. If God has placed a congregation in its time and place for the purpose of extending the kingdom of God, then none of the above measurements can help us discern if we are, in fact, achieving that call.

The question that helps define your focus is simply this one: "What would you be willing to go out of business for?"

Handt Hanson was attending an annual Christmas breakfast at a large convention center in the Twin Cities. He was at a large table hosted by a friend. In the conversation that preceded the program, one of those at the table learned that Handt was the Director of Worship at Prince of Peace. In hearing that, the man challenged Handt's leadership in contemporary worship. When Handt explained that it was about reaching out to another generation or two to invite people into a living relationship with the Savior, Jesus Christ, the man replied, "But what does that have to do with being Lutheran? At our church we've decided that we will continue to do traditional Lutheran worship until the last person shuts out the lights."

While we may disagree with that person's sense of mission, he clearly had focus. And because he and the other members of his congregation had focus, they invested in their particular understanding of the call to their congregation. This was their particularity!

# Momentum

The second mundane miracle of God in the church is momentum. Momentum is achieved when the "particularity" of a ministry is clearly defined and the organization and resources of that ministry line up in support of that focus. Energy is created in momentum. One person's sense of contributing to the greater good of the ministry of that congregation is contagious, and another picks it up and adds his or her efforts to it.

I call this the spiritual multiplication principle. This principle suggests that wherever energy is most visibly and emotionally engaging, it will draw to itself the energy of others. In some cases, this is the negative energy of complaint and blaming. But when it is the positive energy of focus, the results are impressive.

At Prince of Peace, for example, the energy of the above exercise has already created a comparable energy in a variety of our ministry leaders. They are already asking the question, "How does this advance one of our key themes?" And if the answer is that it doesn't, the question is simple: "Why would we do it?" If the answer is that it clearly lends support for one of the key themes, then the next question is, "How soon can we begin to implement this activity, and how many others can we engage in doing it?"

That's momentum. Momentum is the Holy Spirit's power at work in and through a number of people engaged in a variety of activities and efforts. But these are all aligned to the greater direction of the ministry provided by its defined focus.

For example, one of our key themes is "Connections." As a large congregation, it is easy for some people to come and participate in our ministries and not be identified or even personally welcomed. For some this is, in fact, a gift. When visitors come from an experience of wounding in another congregation, we can provide the healing that anonymity alone can give. But sooner or later, such persons will either become engaged at Prince of Peace or leave for another ministry. Our deepest fear is that they will heal and then simply drift into inactivity.

We want Prince of Peace to be a congregation of connections—with God and one another. So, one of my key objectives is to *create a culture of "three touches."* By that I mean that no one should enter the campus and leave their car for any reason without three people greeting them, welcoming them, and asking if they can be of assistance. In order to accomplish this, I will need to recruit and equip staff to be front line "welcomers"—especially during the week. Next, I will need to equip our hospitality leader to understand that her job is to create a large team of "touchers"

> *Create a culture of "three touches."*

around any of the ministries and events at Prince of Peace. Last, I will need to engage our disciples in behaviors of appropriate "touch."

Not long ago, I asked the disciples gathered in worship to greet and meet at least three people in worship that they didn't know. I told them that, if they were like me, just the first name would do because, by the end of the worship, that would be all I could remember. The congregation erupted in a moment of "heavenly chaos." But I wasn't finished. At the end of the worship service, I asked them to wave at those they'd met as they left and simply say, "I hope to see you next week!" For over two weeks I received feedback from our disciples on how wonderful that experience was.

The point was to begin the process of equipping our disciples to be the presence of Jesus in a "three-touch" culture. I am aware that it will take time and repetition—but if we are to advance the key objective of "three touches" for the sake of creating a community of connections, it will be worth it. This is focus at work creating momentum.

# A Praying Board

All of this is the result of a praying board. As I previously mentioned, our church board meets once a month and begins each meeting with a senior pastor's Bible study. The point is this: we are actively committed to growing deeper in Jesus Christ together. Our conviction is that this is the only way we can effectively lead our missional, disciple-making ministry.

This is based on the prelude to Acts 16—the events in Acts 13. In Acts 13 we read about the charge given to Barnabas and Saul. But the commissioning of these two as apostles grew out of a gifted and praying (worshiping) board. We read:

> Now in the church at Antioch here were prophets and teachers; Barnabas, Simeon who was called Niger, Lucius of Cyrene, Manaen a member of the court of Herod the ruler, and Saul. While they were worshiping the Lord and fasting, the Holy Spirit said, "Set apart for me Barnabas and Saul for the work to which I have called them." Then after fasting and praying they laid their hands on them and sent them off. (Acts 13:1-3)

Please note that they heard the call of God as "*they were worshiping the Lord and fasting.*" That means that they were in prayer. Also note that once they had become convinced of the call of God to set apart Barnabas and Saul, they didn't stop praying and worshiping. Instead, they continued, and only after more of that spiritual work did they obey the call of God.

There was a testing of the call. The focus for action was to be affirmed by more prayer and, I assume, conversation with one another. But the gifts of God had led these leaders to this time and place for this particular action. And it would advance the kingdom of God beyond their hopes and dreams!

How do you elect your board or church council? Ours is a board made up of gifted persons who must feel called to serve in this capacity. The key word there is "called." To lead the ministry of Christ's church is so much more than business, though it includes that!—and legislation—though that may be a part of it. The call to lead our ministries is a selection process that ought to include a gifts assessment of both what is needed and who has those gifts for the sake of advancing the particular call of God in that place and time.

Once this is in place, then surely we will discern what God wants our ministries to be. The question is not what we want but what God calls us to be about, as best we can discern it. That means the primary purpose of leaders is to grow deeper in our discipleship together and pray for God's leading. That's the model of Acts 13.

That morning when Elaine and Lynette challenged me, I had to take it seriously. Why? Because I believe that God has called them to leadership on our board. It wasn't because of a popularity contest masquerading as an election. Prayer, commitment to practicing the Marks of Discipleship, and the exercising of key gifts led them to serve on our board. The result isn't perfect—but neither was Paul's or Barnabas' ministry! But I dare to believe it will better empower me to lead for the sake of God's kingdom.

An enormous amount of time in many of our church council meetings is spent in discussing the problems and shortfalls of budget or failed expectations. These may be important, but they often become the only important business. A perfunctory nod is given to the spiritual nature of our work by a brief devotion given by a member, followed by a short, obligatory prayer. There is little time spent in listening to God or growing in our understanding and application of the power of God's word and the Holy Spirit. No wonder the mundane miracles of focus and momentum are so rare!

**The point of Acts 13:1-3 is simply this: disciples must take more time and be in conversation and prayer with one another more often when making critical decisions that can shape the future of the church.**

So, make your church council a praying body of believers. Invite them to grow in faith so that they can lead the ministry of the congregation to grow others in faith. Limit the time spent on busy-ness. Unleash the power of spiritual purpose by asking the question of particularity: Why has God put us in this place and time? What does God expect of us? How will we know if we are doing it?

Saul (Paul) and Barnabas surely had a clear sense of their mission. The voyage they took and the witness they made on Cyprus confirm this. And this was the prelude to the unleashing of passion in the life and ministry of Paul that we can now turn to.

# Vision

"How many of you often drive by a church that just a generation or two ago had a thriving ministry?" I asked. Nearly all of our disciple leaders raised their hands. "Have you ever wondered what happened?" I asked, and saw some nodding of heads. "Let me suggest that the reason their ministry has shrunk in upon itself is a lack of vision. It's not that they didn't have a vital vision at one time. Of course they did. Rather, it is that, having achieved that vision, they never took the time to recast the vision for their ministries."

I definitely had their attention now. "That's why we are here together tonight," I continued. "At Prince of Peace our mission remains the same: To increase and deepen the living discipleship (Marks of Discipleship) of those affiliated with Prince of Peace. In other words, we exist to share *real faith for their real lives*. But I want to share with you a new vision that calls our disciple-making ministry into a future that fits with the changing real world around us." Then we began a vision-led process.

Vision is not a static thing. In fact, I have come to believe that an effective and compelling vision in the twenty-first century is probably good for about five years. Then the process of re-visioning must occur. Sometimes this re-visioning is part of an intentional reassessing. More often than not, however, it is the result of ministries that just are not working—especially ones that once did. This is exactly the problem that Paul and his companions face in Acts 16:6-10.

Paul and his companions are led by a vision for ministry to the people of the Roman province of Asia (what we now know as Turkey). Their vision leads them initially through the provinces of Phrygia and Galatia. But, for whatever reason, we read that they were *"forbidden by the Holy Spirit to speak the word in Asia."* Not easily deterred, Paul and his companions continue to travel north and we read: *"When they had come opposite Mysia, they attempted to go into Bithynia, but the Spirit of Jesus did not allow them; so, passing by Mysia, they went down to Troas"* (Acts 16:7-8).

# Frustration: God's Doorway to the Future

Can you imagine how frustrated Paul must have been? We cannot help but believe, given everything we know of Paul in the New Testament, that he and his companions were convinced that God was leading them to preach the gospel in Asia. But twice circumstances intervened that made this vision impossible to achieve. Luke isn't interested in giving us the details of these "spiritual blocks." The reason is simple—they aren't the point. The point is that God is at work here.

We cannot know Paul and believe that this great missionary accepted these hindrances easily. A cursory overview of his courage and persistence—as well as how often he speaks of learning patience at the hands of endurance—clearly shows his impatience for the spread of the gospel.

So, Paul's frustration level must have been at a high intensity by the time he has ended up in Troas. Paul and his companions have taken a road not planned and arrived at a destination not anticipated. Sounds like ministry in the twenty-first century, doesn't it?!

Vision—a big enough vision for Christ's church in a particular time and place—will be tested before it is defined. That's what is happening to Paul and his companions. It's not his mission that is being tested. It is his understanding of how and where and with whom that mission will next be accomplished that is being tested.

One of the great discipleship lessons in the book of Acts is that all worthy efforts will be tested. That is to say that those who follow the calling of Jesus and give of their lives to advance God's kingdom will be tested. Our resolve will be tested. The selection of our companions will be tested, as it was for Paul and Barnabas around John Mark's participation in this missionary venture (see Acts 15:36-40). Our commitment to the mission and the vision will be tested.

But such spiritual refining is necessary for us to be open to the call of God. The frustration levels of Paul and his companions will, in fact, create the openness for God's calling and the vision that will lead them forward. God has been active within these disciples to create an inner urgency to receive the new vision. And God has actively moved them precisely to where they can best launch out in fulfillment of the new vision.

I was frustrated. I remembered a psychologist years ago defining frustration as "anger in the gut and confusion in the head." I can't remember his name. But I still remember his definition because it works. And I was frustrated.

On the one hand, we were growing in excitement and effectiveness in so many of the areas of our ministry. On the other hand, it was increasingly clear that we needed to implement staff cuts because our *Journey of Faith* contributions were coming to an end, and the overall giving hadn't risen to support the added staff.

The question that kept coming to me was this: If we have a God of abundance (and we do!), why aren't we experiencing that abundance in support of our staff? After wrestling with this for a number of nights, it dawned on me: We might be wrongly staffed. If so, how can we discern a "rightly staffed" ministry? As I continued to pray, I began to understand some of the initial steps necessary to rightly staff our ministry. My heart ached when I realized that one of the staff members I respected and liked the most was in a position that was unnecessary. Then I began to think that with the help of the board and the executive staff team, we would have to engage in a thorough evaluation of all of our staff. And we did.

The result is that we know where we are staffed well. We also know where we are not staffed rightly and where questions remain. But the board members during our visioning retreat affirmed the process. One member said, "We're like the *Titanic*." Then, seeing our shocked expressions, he continued, "but we won't sink because we have a captain who listens to us." (Whew!) His point was that the hard work was being responsibly and compassionately done in order to move toward the new vision for Prince of Peace.

Frustration had opened me to ideas I had not considered. My inner struggle had opened my heart and mind to a process that was foreign to me. And God had already supplied the lay and staff leadership to creatively and supportively help us move through Phrygia and Galatia, past

Mysia and to Troas—a destination I had never considered reaching. God was at work, again.

# How Vision Comes

Just 20 years ago it would have been difficult to find the word vision in relationship to leadership. But in the intervening years, with the upheaval in our society, the word vision has been attached to leadership in order to differentiate those leaders who can lead an organization through difficult times and secure its future. Visionary leadership is the term for such leaders. Visionary leadership includes a number of elements. Among them is the ability to catch sight of a future that is compelling enough to engage and energize followers. Paul was a visionary leader.

Our text continues with these words: *"During the night Paul had a vision: there stood a man of Macedonia pleading with him and saying, 'Come over to Macedonia and help us.' When he had seen the vision, we immediately tried to cross over to Macedonia, being convinced that God had called us to proclaim the good news to them"* (Acts 16:9-10).

Vision comes to the leader. I know of no compelling and sustaining vision that has emerged from a group or committee. Yet many of us in ministry expect the vision for our kingdom building to simply bubble up from the rich soil of the community. It just doesn't happen that way. The vision came to Paul—not to Paul and his companions.

> Vision comes to the leader. I know of no compelling and sustaining vision that has emerged from a group or committee.

If disciple leaders are to catch sight of God's vision for their ministries, it will be through the process suggested in this marvelous text. First, there will be a growing frustration with what is the current reality. This growing frustration creates a sense of urgency. Something is holding the ministry back and blocking the community's participation in growing the kingdom of God.

This is where we need Luke's perspective. Many of us will spend enormous amounts of energy defining the problem. Luke spends no time explaining why Paul and his companions were blocked from fulfilling their vision to preach in Asia. Instead, they continue to work toward that goal. These efforts result in a change of focus—from the blocks themselves—to a new future. Luke's perspective is that knowing what isn't working will not help us move ahead. What is necessary is to begin to look for a new future. Paul's dream emerges from his frustration—a frustration that causes him to struggle to find a future for his mission.

Let disciples spend less time defining the problem and more effort on seeking and acting toward a future ministry that is worth their lives. How many of us are weighed down by a set of problems that we just never get past? The way through them is to prayerfully seek a new focus for ministry. Instead of Asia, we need to seek God's Macedonia.

Disciple leaders will need to be in ministry and conversation with those who follow as they seek the future to which God will call them. This serving and listening will become the rich soil from which God will draw out a new ministry vision. Without this mutual serving, the leader has little credibility. Unless the leader is listening, he or she will be drawn by a vision that may or may not include the community of followers. But as we serve and converse together, as Paul and his companions surely did, we begin to grow together. Then our frustrations are shared. Experiencing a shared frustration is critical because it builds the urgency necessary for change. When this shared frustration is linked to the call of God to mission, the community is ready to receive a new vision and the leader is prepared to seek that new vision.

The leader will need to take time away from the congregation and her or his daily work. Like Paul, whose sleep created this break, we need a spiritual space to imagine and hear the voice of the Holy Spirit. Our focus should be upon the new opportunities in our context. How is the congregation positioned for effective ministry? What might better position the community of faith for outreach and service? Are there populations that have emerged to which we might reach out? If so, then we want to imagine what it would look like to be in that ministry.

The vision of Paul is also instructive because it affirms that the content of our mission doesn't change. But the context might. On the one hand, this change of context may mean that we will have to move geographically or perhaps join with another faith community for more effective ministry. A change of context could mean, on the other hand, reaching out in service to a new constituency in our community.

One congregation was moved by a vision to reach out to the needs of young families that were moving into their established neighborhood. As an older congregation (average age was just under sixty), they knew that they would have to think beyond their previous programming. In order to re-imagine, they began to talk to their children and grandchildren about the needs of twenty-first-century families. Their first attempts at outreach were not particularly successful. Then they retooled their ministry with the addition of a day care center and an invitation for a parent's night out. The church hired the appropriate staff and on one Friday a month provided a safe and socially active place for children so that their parents could have time together. A young couple emerged as leaders and were supported in developing a new ministry specifically to young families. This new vision was costly. The congregation had to stop doing what it was comfortable doing and take a risk. The vision, however, was understood as the difference between life or death. Either the congregation experienced rebirth, or, the members believed, it would die with the aging of its members. Their context and their willingness to have conversation to discover ways to effectively minister to the needs of their community have paid off.

Vision is always needs-based. The needs that the vision addresses, however, are not those of the ones already there. Paul's dream was the call to meet the needs of the Macedonians—not to better meet his needs. So, vision is externally focused. But this external focus is what creates mission. God blesses the church in mission—not the congregation of the status quo. But when God lifts up a vision for ministry beyond ourselves, then our deepest needs are met.

The vision comes to the leader in a clear and compelling picture of the future. The above vision is a simple attempt to share a compelling future for the ministry of Prince of Peace. But notice, it doesn't talk a lot about the "how" of it. That can only be learned as we actively pursue the vision. Paul's dream didn't specify how he and his companions would get to Macedonia, where they would start, or even who would necessarily be involved. The call was clear and compelling and simple: "Come over and help us."

# Sharing the Vision

Once Paul had the dream, he shared it with his companions. This is the first point of risk for disciples in community. No leader has the right to impose his or her vision on a community of faith. The vision is shared,

> If other leaders catch this vision, it has been confirmed for that church.

and we must trust the Holy Spirit to have created a heart for the vision in the community. Not all will necessarily catch the vision. But if other leaders do, then the vision has been confirmed for that church.

If the vision is compelling to the leader but not to the congregation, then the leader is being called elsewhere. I have found few conflicts that cannot be resolved through conversation and negotiation in the church. But a conflict of vision is one of them. The reason is simple: you cannot go two places simultaneously. One destination will have to be sacrificed for the sake of another. Compelling vision creates energy. Any disciple who sets aside such a vision will experience the ennui that follows. Disciples are called to mission. Walking away from a clear vision of that calling will be disheartening—no matter how we rationalize it.

But if the vision is shared and accepted by the community, two wonderful things are created. The first is the restoration of purpose, and the second is deeper community.

When moving from a Membership-Model ministry to a disciple-making one, the energy released is palpable. In the example above, a renewed sense of purpose moved through the leadership and then the congregation as a whole. This purpose provided the direction the congregation needed. A new purpose will, however, be costly. Some will choose to leave the congregation because they simply disagree with the new vision. Others will burn out in their zealousness to accomplish the vision immediately. Both are confirmations that the congregation is actively engaged in mission.

One of the most painful aspects of growth in our churches is the loss of our members. This is painful because many of those who leave because of a renewed purpose will be among the past leadership. Their leaving may simply be a witness to being overinvested in the past. Leaders who move from membership to discipleship in their ministries will need to build a bridge to the future to minimize the loss of people. We do this by inviting as many as possible to the journey as often as possible. Our goal is to celebrate the past but build from it into a new future worthy of the efforts already invested in our past. Most ministries have been successful because of the efforts and sacrifices of saints in the past. We want to affirm and honor that. But we claim their spirit of giving to move into God's future.

On the other hand, I have come to realize that there are good reasons for people to leave our congregations. As painful as it is to say goodbye to some, if they cannot support the new vision, they need another place in which they can serve and grow. I have watched Christians who were disruptive and blocking in one congregation move into a new church and become actively and positively supportive and engaged. For some it will always be easier to adopt a new agenda in a new congregation than to accept the new vision in the ministry in which they have been so involved.

On the other side of a vision is the formation of community. The text reads: "*When he had seen the vision, **we** immediately tried to cross over to Macedonia, being convinced that God had called **us** to proclaim the good news to them*" (Acts 16:10, emphasis added).

I am aware that many scholars refer to this passage as one of the "we" passages in the book of Acts. They suggest that this is when Luke joins Paul and his companions. That may be true. What is more compelling about this text is, however, the ownership of the vision.

The second point of risk for the leader in sharing the vision is when the community of faith "owns" the vision. There comes a time when the vision will be adopted and claimed by the community. When that time occurs, the leader must relinquish the vision. It no longer belongs to her or him. More than that, it will be taken in directions that the leader had not imagined. But that is our prayer! When this happens, focus has created momentum. The large vision has made room for all the "smaller" visions of those in the community who can add to the ministry through their gifts and talents. Leaders who cannot let go of the vision and affirm those who strive, in their unique ways, to advance that vision will become blocks to the mission of the church.

Not long ago, a former colleague in ministry at Prince of Peace helped form a Peace with Justice Ministry. When I heard about it, I was somewhat surprised. But, after speaking with him and hearing both his commitment to discipleship and his passion for this ministry, I concluded I needed to get out of the way. Over time, I watched as discipleship initiatives for recycling and global warming emerged. I watched as committed disciples gathered to quietly advance constructive efforts for responsible stewardship of creation and life on planet earth. My decision to prayerfully get out of the way has been confirmed by a growing discipleship ministry that hasn't gotten sidetracked at all. Instead, some of our disciple members have found a place where their passions and gifts advance our vision of *A Church for the World and the World in a Church*. Visionary leadership means letting go at times.

My suspicion is that Paul let go as well. I believe that the insight of Paul's leadership is that he was willing to trust others with their gifts. I don't know if Paul sought the ship and made the decisions about leaving for Macedonia or not, but I doubt it. Community is created when a compelling vision is large enough to embrace the particular visions of other disciples and still move forward.

When disciple leaders share their vision, they lose control of that vision. If the vision is compelling, God will use the gifts and passions of others to take that vision and accomplish more than the leader could have imagined. The role of the leader is to cheer such efforts on and to celebrate them.

The leader also must translate "failures" into "great learning." When Paul received the vision to go to Macedonia, it wasn't coincidence that had moved him and his companions to Troas—a port city opposite Macedonia! Paul's role was, at that point, to celebrate the vision and recast the previous failures to go into Asia as the hand of God leading them to Troas. When we find ourselves in places we had never anticipated, we ought to immediately look for the heaven-sent opportunity before us. God has not been inactive. A critical leadership function in our time of chaos and change is to transform the "failure" experience into a "great learning" experience.

Dr. Lee Griffin, a Christian psychiatrist and mentor of mine, once told me, "All life learning comes from pain. The tragedy is," he continued, "that not all pain leads to life learning."

He was right. The greatest lessons we learn in life are rarely from our successes. They are usually from our greatest experiences of failure, challenge, or tragedy. The real sorrow of the soul is when such pain does not lead to great learning. The disciple leader will always strive to translate experiences of failure into learning. Failure demoralizes. Learning equips. Tragedy turns us into ourselves. Seeing the hand of God in these experiences opens us to life again.

# It's about People and God's Love

"If you could express the one purpose of discipleship at Prince of Peace, what would you say?"

The question was asked in a group of pastors. I had to think. No one had challenged me with such a singularity before. After I had pondered for a while, I remember saying, "I don't know if this is the answer to the question I'll have tomorrow, but today I think I'd say this. The single purpose of discipleship is to connect people in confidence to the love of God in Jesus Christ.

"Now," I continued, "having said that, let me tell you what I mean." And the room erupted in laughter. "No," I said, "seriously. What I mean is that most personal or family crises occur at a time and an hour when the pastor and congregation are simply not around. In that moment, if the individual or family members are disciples of Jesus, then they will know the presence of God for them. And if it is a family crisis, they can be the presence of Jesus for one another until the church can be present in others."

The point is that it's all about God's grace and the people of God's grace. When we understand that, then we will quickly understand that we cannot be a people of God's grace and keep it to ourselves.

I remember watching her come down the center aisle at Prince of Peace. The last worship service had just concluded, and I was tired. I was gathering up my papers and puppet to leave when I looked up and saw her. I watched as she knelt at the altar rail and wept. I looked around hoping that another disciple of Jesus would see her and reach out to her. When that didn't happen, I put my stuff down and quietly approached her. Kneeling in front of her, I gently placed my hand on her forearm and asked, "Is anything wrong? Can I help you?"

She looked up and smiled. "No, Pastor Mike, nothing is wrong at all. I'm crying because I'm so happy. I've been gone from church for a long time, and I don't know why, but I decided to come here today . . ." she paused and continued, "and Jesus met me here."

"Well," I said with a smile, "thank God for that. The Holy Spirit was at work."

"But Pastor Mike," she said, "would you pray for me? Pray that I'll come back and that I'll have the strength to share with my friends what happened. None of them believe in God, and I want to be able to tell them what happened here today." So, we bowed our heads and prayed for faith and strength and courage to share.

When God shows up in our lives, we experience grace at a profound level. But we cannot claim that grace and keep it to ourselves. I was surprised by that young woman's candor, but not by her prayer request. When we are met by the Holy Spirit, God has created a holy moment and a sacred memory. We need courage to share that with others precisely because it is so special to us. We need strength to live from the memory into a new season of life—just like she was longing for. We need to return to worship in the presence of the living God. This is what renewed vision and mission is all about. God will create within disciples the willingness to follow Jesus and to witness. That's what happened in Acts 16.

There is one last aspect of this dream of Paul's that we need to discuss. The outcome of their following the dream was the most successful mission experience in Paul's life. Paul tells us of this marvel in 2 Corinthians 8:1-5.

> We want you to know, brothers and sisters, about the grace of God that has been granted to the churches of Macedonia; for during a severe ordeal of affliction, their abundant joy and their extreme poverty have overflowed in a wealth of generosity on their part. For, as I can testify, they voluntarily gave according to their means, and even beyond their means, begging us earnestly for the privilege of sharing in this ministry to the saints—and this, not merely as we expected; they gave themselves first to the Lord and, by the will of God, to us.

On the other side of a great vision for mission is the promise of lives changed. That's what happened when Paul and his companions received and acted upon the vision that God had given them. This is the promise of Christ to disciples who dare to re-imagine in the power of the Holy Spirit. But the promise is received as we not only dare to dream of God's church but also, then, to live our way into that dream. This obedient living leads to renewed ministry, the outcome of which is a blessing to the world and the kingdom of God that we can only hope to achieve. And, with the blessings of God will come the insight to see and claim those blessings. Paul's vision to enter Macedonia resulted in a harvest of personal blessings, as this passage of 2 Corinthians tells us. More than that, it multiplied those blessings for the saints in Jerusalem—and served as an example to others to turn outward in giving.

# Tithing and Beyond

Sooner or later the life of faith will produce generosity. In our materialistic world, this is a necessary conversation for disciples to have with one another. This shouldn't surprise us, because even in the world of Corinth materialism was apparently a significant deterrent to generous giving. The Membership Model has reduced Christian generosity to dues paying. In this old model our giving is directly related to what we, as members, will benefit from. If the roof leaks, our membership is enhanced by repairing the leak. When ministry lags, giving to uphold that ministry adds value to the benefits we as members receive. The problem is that this perspective has nothing to do with a biblical view of giving.

The Bible teaches us to give—a tithe specifically—for two reasons. The first is out of gratitude to God. The second is because our giving increases our participation in the blessings of God. When Paul began his collection of sacrificial gifts for the famine-ravaged Jerusalem church, he understood this as an opportunity to grow in the first-century Christians' trusting of God to provide for them. His underlying principle was simply: We cannot out-give God.

This reflects the teaching in Malachi 3:8-12:

> Will anyone rob God? Yet you are robbing me! But you say, "How are we robbing you?" In your tithes and offerings! You are cursed with a curse, for you are robbing me—the whole nation of you! Bring the full tithe into the storehouse, so that there may be food in my house, and thus put me to the test, says the LORD of hosts; see if I will not open the windows of heaven for you and pour down for you an overflowing blessing. I will rebuke the locust for you, so that it will not destroy the produce of your soil; and your vine in the field shall not be barren, says he LORD of hosts. Then all nations will count you happy, for you will be a land of delight, says the LORD of hosts.

When I entered the ministry I was serving as an associate pastor in Spokane, Washington. I remember being appointed to three standing committees: youth, evangelism, and stewardship. At my first stewardship committee meeting I informed the team that I wouldn't preach a stewardship sermon—period. They accepted this from their new pastor in stunned silence!

A few months later, the church treasurer followed me out into the parking lot after the council meeting. "Pastor Mike," he said, "you don't tithe, do you?"

"No, I don't," I replied. When he asked me why, I told him that I didn't believe in it. I found no biblical support for this legalistic requirement. To which he responded, "If I could show you where the Bible teaches tithing, would you do it?" And I said I would.

A week or so later I received a note from Ted and a list of Bible passages, including the one above. I read them—then shared them with my wife,

Chris. We concluded that God clearly commanded us to tithe. We looked at our giving and discovered that we were giving at about a 4 percent to 5 percent level. It took us between three and five years to reach a tithe, but we did it—even with two small children and a modest salary.

I have been grateful to that lay leader ever since. What I have discovered is the blessing of faithful giving. It has nothing to do with getting more money from what I give. Instead, it has to do with growing my heart. My wife and I have discovered that tithing has taught us how to better manage our money—and our appetites! More than that, we have found joy in being able to give beyond a tithe.

Not long ago, my wife—the realist in our family!—looked at me and said, "You know, the more we give the more we seem able to give." She's right. God has kept the promise of opening the floodgates of heaven to us.

Tithing is the foundation for our giving—not the ceiling. Almost all of the tithers I know give more than that out of gratitude to God and in order to meet specific needs. The result is not necessarily a greater income. It does produce within the disciple a heart of gratitude and a perspective of blessing. Most of the disciples I know who tithe wouldn't give it up for anything. Unfortunately, most of those who do not tithe still have a firm grip on what they have, at the expense of what God would give them. Only open hands can receive the blessings of heaven. It's not that the blessings aren't available to all. But with fists hanging on tightly to what we have, we cannot grasp the blessings all around us.

> Tithing is the foundation for our giving—not the ceiling.

Membership is all about hanging on to what I have and demanding what I think the organization owes me. Discipleship is all about acknowledging that God owns it all and has graciously given to us all that we have. God allows us to hold onto 90 percent and return to God 10 percent. When we are obedient to this command, we open ourselves to the life-changing generosity of God. That's when we desire to give. As God blesses us, we look to become blessings from God in the lives of others.

I also want to point out that the word "joy" (the NRSV translates the Malachi text as "happy") is used in both the Second Corinthians text and the Malachi text. The point is that our generosity creates joy within us. The truth of the matter is that I have met many misers in my life, but I have never met a "happy" or joyful miser. But I have met countless people who tithe and speak of their joy in doing so. Generous lives are lives that see, claim, and share the abundance of God.

If you are not tithing, let me challenge you to grow into a tithe. Look at what you give and see what percent of your take-home pay it is. Then make a plan to grow at a 1 percent to 3 percent per year rate. Follow through on the plan. Then, when you reach a tithe, celebrate and give thanks to God. I urge you to continue that tithe for at least three years. At the end of those three years, ask what changes your disciplined giving has created within you. I know you will be surprised.

One caveat is necessary. Sometimes circumstances intervene and we are unable to tithe. Trust God's grace in those circumstances and ask God to lead you through and into a time when you can, once again, give as you'd planned. The call to tithing is not a punitive one. God asks us to give from what we have, not from what we do not have.

Disciples tithe out of gratitude for God's blessings. And, in the economy of the Holy Spirit, those very blessings grow a generosity that will move us joyfully beyond the tithe.

# Questions and Reflections

1. Have you ever experienced frustration becoming a doorway to God's future? What happened?

2. Discuss with a group of other disciples whether they have experienced God's vision in their lives? Ask them if it was in response to a growing need or frustration.

3. Do you agree with the idea that vision comes from a leader to the group but, once shared is owned by all and will be taken further than the leader could have originally imagined? Have you seen this happen?

4. Have you experienced the power of focus and momentum? Is your congregation thriving on these two mundane miracles of the Holy Spirit? If not, what might be done to achieve focus and grow momentum?

5. Are you tithing or willing to grow to a tithe? Have you shared your financial generosity with a friend or family so that they could celebrate with you? Is tithing understood in your congregation as the ceiling or foundation for Christian giving?

# V I

---

# The Power of Purpose—Acts 28

We discover the will of God for our lives by living. By that I mean to suggest that few of us simply "land" in our life's purpose once and for all. I have had many Christians ask how they could know the will of God for their lives. My experience and reading of the Bible suggests that God's will calls us into life and invites continuous discovery. The metaphor for this is a river. At the source it appears to be more like a rivulet; but, as it winds its way under the force of gravity, it will join with other bodies of water and perhaps even go underground at times. But it eventually ends up in the sea. Our lives wind around events and activities. We will join with the lives of others for a season and, at times, even go underground when we feel lost or move into a private time. But for the Christian there is the confidence that we will finally enter into the complete will of God forever. We discover the will of God for our lives as we walk with God in faith daily.

So, it is not surprising that the journey of Paul from persecutor of Christians to foremost missionary of this fledgling movement will take him from Antioch to Jerusalem, Macedonia, and, eventually, Rome. Only as we can follow and then reflect on his life as a devout Jew, born a Roman citizen, then on to prestige in Jerusalem can we see how God could make use of the various threads of his life to bring him to the center of the world: Rome. By appealing his case to the Emperor, a right of every Roman citizen, his journey's destination was set. But for the reader of Acts, this would seem to have been his destiny all along.

So often we, as disciples, forget that faith is the active pursuit of life in trust of God. We would like a road map. We would like to know the destination of our purpose. And as leaders in ministry we tend to come to our participation and roles in the congregation with a similar set of expectations. Yet, a congregation's purpose will be revealed over time. We meet the Holy Spirit as we are willing to discover the "new" calling of ministry in our ever-changing world. If Paul had not been open to the vision in Acts 16, or if he had been content to remain in Antioch all along, the purpose for which his life was destined would not have been discovered.

The question is whether we are open to this spiritual discovery of the will of God in our lives and ministries again and again. But the commitment to mission is at the heart of our willingness to rediscover and refocus. The mission is the proclamation, in word and deed, of the good news of Jesus' crucifixion and resurrection. To the degree that we are willing to apply this mission to whatever time and circumstances in which we find ourselves, we will continue the wonderful journey into the will of God.

# Persistence: Commitment to Purpose

In Acts 28 we discover Paul nearing the end of his journey to Rome. The commitment to mission to the Gentiles, according to Luke, became crystal clear in Corinth. In Corinth, Paul turns away from active missionary work among his Jewish brothers and sisters to the singular pursuit of Gentile converts. This does not mean that he will not have Jewish Christian friends and associates. Nor does it mean that he will no longer witness to Jews if the possibility presents itself. What it clarified for Paul was the focus of his ministry in terms of *whom* he would address. This was the point when, looking back on his life, we could guess that God would eventually call him to go to Rome.

Jerusalem was the center of Judaism. All Jews, no matter where they were in the Roman Empire, looked to Jerusalem as their religious home.

For Gentiles in the Roman Empire, Rome was the center of the universe. The saying "all roads lead to Rome" was an indication of its stature as the community for a man who knew he was called to a ministry of missionary work among the Gentiles. In Acts 18, Paul turns his heart and soul from Jerusalem to Rome—though unknowingly.

We read:

> After this Paul left Athens and went to Corinth . . . When Silas and
> Timothy arrived from Macedonia, Paul was occupied with proclaiming

the word, testifying to the Jews that the Messiah was Jesus. When they opposed and reviled him, in protest he shook the dust from his clothes and said to them, "Your blood be on your own heads! I am innocent. From now on I will go to the Gentiles." Then he left the synagogue and went to the house of a man named Titius Justus, a worshiper of God; his house was next door to the synagogue. . . . One night the Lord said to Paul in a vision, "Do not be afraid, but speak and do not be silent; for I am with you, and no one will lay a hand on you to harm you, for there are many in this city who are my people." He stayed there a year and six months, teaching the word of God among them. (Acts 18:1, 5-7, 9-11)

In this text we see the clarity of focus that will typify Paul's journeys from this time forward. Through praise and condemnation, Paul's persistence will drive him forward and create the person we meet in his letters.

I once was told of a commencement address by the great leader and statesman Winston Churchill. When it came time for him to address the graduates of a prestigious university in England, he got up, looked out on the crowd who were eagerly awaiting his words, said, "Never give up." And then took his seat. As everyone sat in stunned silence, Churchill got up again and simply said, "Never give up." He would return to the rostrum once more to say those same three words. That was the sum total of his speech.

I don't know if the story is factual. I do know that in the deepest sense it is true. What is true about the story at the very least is the insight into the character of this great leader. In the dark days of the Nazi bombing of Britain, it was this indomitable spirit, this persistence, that kept the fire of freedom burning in that nation. No wonder the national symbol of England is the bulldog.

Paul will demonstrate the same persistence in his mission to the Gentiles.

What is persistence? I have come to believe that persistence is patience with a purpose. Patience without a purpose is simply biding our time. Purpose without patience is nothing more than wishful thinking or, at best, wasted energy. The great goals in life can only be achieved through clarity of purpose and patience to work through time and circumstance.

> **Persistence is patience with a purpose.**

Disciples understand the need for persistence as we discover, again and again, the mission of the church in new times and situations. It takes persistence to remain committed to the gospel of Jesus Christ in a time of paradoxes. The polarities of spiritual hunger and skepticism provide challenging boundaries for our ministry. The paradox of distrust of religion and pursuit of spirituality will confront any leader who is committed to the Lord of the church and the church that he founded. How do we become non-institutional while, at the same time, being responsible for the institutional forms of our congregations? In an age of caricature, when the extremes of religion in the world dominate the perceptions of those inside and outside the Christian church, how do we present ourselves authentically and with integrity? It takes persistence.

The call to discipleship is the greatest call in the history of the world—but it is not easy. The call to be the church in the world is a call to be in the one institution that can have the greatest impact on our world for good—but it will not be easy. Disciple leaders will have to consciously choose to do what is best, not what is easy. That's why I have come to add one more fruit of the Spirit to the list in Galatians: persistence. Only the Holy Spirit can endow us with this spiritual gift.

As we return, now, to Acts 28 we can understand better how Paul can act with such seeming equanimity in the face of threat and acclaim. Paul knows that he is bound for Rome. God has confirmed the call to the Gentiles by calling him to the center of the Gentile world. Paul will patiently pursue his purpose no matter what his circumstances may be.

# Welcome and Setbacks

The first e-mail was a letter of disappointment with our teen ministry. I received it as a copy sent to another staff member. The content of the complaint seemed real so I e-mailed the sender that I would ask the appropriate staff to contact her. That led to a face-to-face conversation between this caring mother and the staff member and his supervisor. Another e-mail was sent to me and I processed it again by referring to the appropriate program staff. That led to a conversation with the staff member, his supervisor, and six to ten couples. The outcome was a reiteration of our mission to make disciples and some key adjustments to our programming. I thought the matter had been appropriately handled and was over. I was wrong.

The next word I heard from the mother was a request for the names of the members of our board. Since this is public information, we, of course, replied with a list of names and phone numbers. Three weeks later I heard that she had had multiple conversations with the members of our church board. Yet, neither she nor they had communicated with me. Then I received a two-page, caustic e-mail attacking me and the direction our ministry was taking.

I was dumbfounded. I had appropriately followed through on her requests. I had kept the door of communication open between her and me. Now, I was being attacked, my motives for ministry impugned, and I was told that the board was not with me.

At the next meeting of the executive board team I shared the e-mail. I had shared, since her family members were long-term members at Prince of Peace and known to many in our congregation, the ongoing response to her legitimate concerns. Now, the issue was no longer between her and me—no matter what the e-mail said. It was between the board and me. So, I asked the executive board team members if now was the time for me to look for service elsewhere. I reiterated that I was committed to disciple-making ministry and that moving in a different direction was within the authority of the board. I would respect that authority. What I would not and could not live with was working in a setting where I didn't know what the board was thinking or where they were. The board executive team members assured me that they agreed with the call to make disciples and reiterated their support for my ministry. They did ask, however, if I would be willing to meet with the letter writer. I said I certainly was open to that and had always been open to that. But, given the content of the e-mail, I would not meet with her alone. And they affirmed that decision.

We called an executive meeting of the board. Once again I shared the process of the past four or five months. Once again I reiterated my commitment to disciple-making ministry and my confidence that, should the board decide that another direction was required, God would lead me to another place of ministry and bless Prince of Peace. The board members sat in silence. Then the conversation began in earnest. What had been said in the e-mail was a distortion of the many conversations the individual had had with board members.

But that wasn't the issue. We often misunderstand or misinterpret what others say to us based on what we want them to say. The issues were: (1) Why was there no communication between the board members and myself during this time? (2) How could we better communicate amongst ourselves so that we could manage this kind of activity in a healthier manner? (3) Why did no one suggest that the individual have a direct conversation with me? (4) What might we learn from this moving forward?

The positive outcomes of that conversation were multiple. First, the board affirmed their commitment to our vision for disciple-making ministry. Second, they affirmed my continued leadership while recognizing that I took seriously my accountability to them. Third, we acknowledged that good people with good intentions can act destructively and provide an opening for the Devil to set us up against one another. Last, we affirmed the practice of resolving conflicts at the lowest possible level.

The conflict was turned into a blessing. We prayed together and a member of the board agreed to have conversation with the individual to provide a board perspective on the mission and vision of Prince of Peace and invite conversation with me. What appeared to be a dead end became a new beginning of openness and candor with the entire board.

In Acts 28, Paul will experience the rapid shifts from hospitality to judgment to unhealthy praise. His clarity of purpose and patient endurance will allow him to navigate these unsettled waters remarkably well. We read:

> After we had reached safety, we then learned that the island was called Malta. The natives showed us unusual kindness. Since it had begun to rain and was cold, they kindled a fire and welcomed all of us around it. Paul had gathered a bundle of brushwood and was putting it on the fire, when a viper, driven out by the heat, fastened itself on his hand. When the natives saw the creature hanging from his hand, they said to one another, "This man must be a murderer; though he has escaped from the sea, justice has not allowed him to live." He, however, shook off the creature into the fire and suffered no harm. They were expecting him to swell up or drop dead, but after they had waited a long time and saw that nothing unusual had happened to him, they changed their minds and began to say that he was a god. (Acts 28:1-6)

Paul, along with the centurion, crew members, other prisoners, and Luke, has been shipwrecked. Paul, who had prophesied that this would happen but that no one would lose his life, was instrumental in bringing them all safely to shore—Acts 27:41-44. Once ashore, they receive the hospitality of the islanders. Wet and cold, the shipwrecked men are welcomed to a hot fire. The warmth of the fire and the kindness of the natives would have proven to be a welcome haven for the storm-tossed, shipwrecked survivors. But it would not last.

Disciple leaders understand this. We know that God provides safe shores for us for a season. There are times, as in the aftermath of the situation with our board members, when we can feel safe and secure. But we know that such time, like that of Paul and his companions, will not last. Sooner or later another issue will emerge, and conflict will ensue.

Twenty-first-century disciples recognize that God will be at work both in our times of comfort and our times of trial. God will give us those seasons of inner peace and outer calm. But God will work in and through our storms to bring us into a closer relationship with him and one another. God will turn our shipwrecks into blessings—just like in Acts 28. For Paul, his ministry was just about to get a welcome boost through the bite of a serpent.

# Snakebit

Paul is helping to keep the others warm and the fire going when the viper bites. His good deed became the occasion for being snakebit! And the natives, who knew that the snake was poisonous, watched and exercised "straight-line thinking."

Straight-line thinking is when we connect the dots between events and the inner character of those experiencing the events. Our thinking follows a straight line from good deeds to good outcomes. Bad deeds or motivations lead to bad outcomes. The problem is that it is often not true. (In this case we see that sometimes even good deeds are seemingly punished.) The natives do not know Paul, let alone his heroic efforts to save the men of that ship. So, they fill in the blanks and judge that he must have been a murderer for "justice" to take away his life after he had been saved from the sea.

Christians as well as those outside the church can suffer from straight-line thinking. Because there is a conflict, someone must have done something wrong. We've already discussed the problem of blame, but this is of a higher magnitude because it suggests the judgment and activity of God. The assumptions are that if no one had done anything wrong, if no one sinned, then everyone would be getting along.

On a personal level, straight-line thinking judges that when someone is experiencing misfortune, they must have earned it. Another way of using straight-line thinking in this arena is when well-intentioned persons say to someone who has experienced tragedy that it was God's will. The implication is that this tragedy was sent by God.

There are times as disciple leaders when we instinctively shift to straight-line thinking. In the above scenario, I did. The first thing that came to my mind was to wonder what I had done wrong. How had I mishandled the situation so that it grew to the size of conflict and became as personal as it did?

But sometimes, the snake just bites. Sometimes conflict or tragedy simply happens. Disciple leaders who understand this will not allow their circumstances to grow out of proportion. Paul did not react to the snakebite. He apparently trusted God to deal with it. At the least, his equanimity disallowed the snakebite to overcome him and dominate his behavior.

Snakebit disciples learn from this. We learn to handle crises and conflict at the lowest possible level. We learn, over time, not to take everything personally—there will be plenty of personal stuff that will come without us making everything personal.

But this can be hard to do when there is a "grain of truth" to the charges, can't it? In Paul's case, look at the judgment of the native: he is a murderer. Well, there is a grain of truth to that, isn't there? Paul was, in fact, a murderer of Christians! But Paul had become so much more since then. Paul had followed the call of Christ and had been set aside for the mission to the Gentiles. Paul wouldn't get hooked by the "grain of truth."

Disciple leaders will learn that the "grain of truth" is usually something from our past that still haunts us. The opportunity is to face it and accept the forgiveness of Jesus Christ that can make us so much more than that. Gossip and false judgments rarely have fangs unless they contain a grain of truth. The problem is that they usually do. That's why we take them so seriously and why they are often passed on.

In the e-mail I received there was a "grain of truth." I am a strong leader. I believe strongly in discipleship as the model for effective ministry in the twenty-first-century Christian church. And I persistently pursue this mission. That means that I do not always take seriously the "membership" complaints of others. The e-mail led me to review my willingness to hear others who disagree with me; beyond that, the e-mail was simply destructive and the sender's behavior sinful.

# Discerning Signal from Noise

Not long ago I met with a wonderful Christian leader. She had been the victim of a change in a congregation's direction because the leadership of that church had not dealt with her with integrity. In that conversation, I asked her if she had any word for me as I sought to lead our congregation through a difficult transition. She thought for a moment and then replied, "Don't believe your own press."

From false accusations of being a murderer, Paul will be hailed as a god. What a roller-coaster ride! From the depth of derision to the height of public acclaim, Paul had experienced it before and was now experiencing it on the island of Malta.

Once again, Luke simply passes over this startling, whiplash change of events. The reason is that Paul had already experienced this with Barnabas earlier in his mission work. The miracles of Paul were not done for his own ends but to serve Jesus Christ. His focus was on the mission of the gospel—not his personal popularity. That provided Paul with the perspective of discerning noise from signal.

Disciple leaders will discover the need to listen selectively. There will be times when the noise level in our lives or ministries will reach a fever pitch. When that happens, we need to take a step out of the noise and begin to try to discern what is really being said; that is, what is the spiritual signal we ought to pay attention to. If we react to the noise, we may get very busy doing many things and never address the real need or problem.

For example, a few months ago I hosted a series of leaders' meetings at Prince of Peace. The purpose was to look at the best of our past, dream about the best possible future for our ministry, and then ask what needed to be achieved or addressed in order to move from the present to the best future, while not losing the best of our past. The response was almost universally positive. But in assembling the many ideas that came out of those meetings, how could I help our leadership differentiate a personal complaint from a real need? In analyzing that, and in conversation with other leaders, I decided that if something was mentioned only once or twice in all these meetings, it was probably noise, not signal. But if something emerged again and again, then we'd better pay attention to it. The issues that were mentioned at every meeting, multiple times, became the basis for the themes and objectives I have shared with you. Now I will take those themes and objectives to the leaders who participated in the earlier meetings and invite them to choose a particular theme for creative problem solving.

We live in a noisy time. In our world we are inundated by the "new" and the "best," resulting in the expectations that we bring to worship and

ministry often being frighteningly high. When our unconscious expectations or identified needs are not being met, we grow impatient and make
noise. Every disciple will need to confront the Membership Model's
legacy of entitlement. In the Membership Model members are entitled to
the best in service and program with few expectations that they are
required to contribute toward these. When more is required or the services of ministry do not satiate this spirit of entitlement, we hear noise.

Discerning noise from signal means responding to what is appropriate
and dismissing what is not. Paul pays no attention, it would seem, to
either the noise of the native's judgments about him or to their false
praise. Instead, Acts 28 moves very quickly into a ministry moment with
the healing of Publius's father.

How do we maintain this clear focus and yet respond to the signals that
are being given? First, listen and collate the noise. Ask yourself and other
disciples what is being said most frequently. Then ask if there is a common need or expectation not being met that is being expressed in the
noise. If so, there's the signal. If not, listen some more—but without getting hooked by the noise. As you listen, pay attention to who is saying
what, and ask yourself if the noise is based on an issue or an emotion. If
it is an issue-based noise, you can then define whether the issue ought to
be confronted, and if so, by whom and in what most constructive way. If
it is an emotional noise, then address it through pastoral care. Effectively
addressing the signal will result in greater energy for mission. Trying to
simply calm all the noise usually ends up in distraction. Distraction rarely
is helpful or constructive. Yet, many of us as disciple leaders are kept
busy minding the noise with little to show for the enormous energy spent
on it.

# Keep on Purpose

Paul navigates the changing tides of public opinion very well. How
does he do it? He keeps on purpose. We read that after Paul healed
Publius's father, *"The rest of the people on the island who had diseases also
came and were cured. They bestowed many honors on us, and when we were
about to sail, they put on board all the provisions we needed"* (Acts 28:9-10).
The point is that even after a very successful ministry to the people of the
islands and the receiving of many honors, Paul's heart was still focused on
Rome. And in the sixteenth verse we read: "When we came into Rome,

Paul was allowed to live by himself, with the soldier who was guarding him" (Acts 28:16). Paul had reached his destination.

The call of discipleship is to live on purpose. We live in the very presence of God. We are invited to live for the eternal love of God made known in Jesus Christ. This shapes the practice of our faith. Only living on purpose can help us not be distracted from our goal of serving Jesus Christ, by either criticisms or praise.

Disciple leaders will have their share of both criticism and praise. On any given Sunday I will receive one or two criticisms of the sermon and, hopefully, more praise. In the past it didn't matter how many compliments I received; I would spend the rest of Sunday, and into the first of the week, fixating on the one or two negatives. The way through this for me was to begin to ask myself two questions. The first was simply, "Did I focus on discipleship and strive to equip my hearers to live their faith?" If the answer was yes, then I could go on. The second question was, "Is there something I need to hear in either the praise or the criticism that will help me preach better?" This question helped me refocus from the hurt of being criticized to the lessons that could be learned.

The problem is this: I have yet to meet a disciple leader who has entered ministry as a pastor or lay leader so they could say no. Most of us entered the mission of the congregation so that we could say yes to others. But systems and responsibilities often require us to say no; that is, to establish appropriate boundaries, policies, and procedures for the sake of order. We need to keep on purpose so that we can say no with the intentionality our mission and vision for ministry requires. And because so many of us have entered ministry to say yes rather than no, we are likely people who want to be liked.

Not long ago I had a conversation with another pastor who was struggling with the critics in his congregation. We both acknowledge that this was a common problem in leading congregations. "But," he said, "everything is going so well. I just don't understand why they can't see that and be more supportive of my ministry."

I laughed and replied, "It sounds as if you'd like them to like you." When he grinned and said that would be nice, I replied, "Well, it took me awhile to understand that not everyone would like me in the church. And frankly, I don't understand it. After all, I'm one of the most likeable people I've ever met!"

The point is that leaders in every sphere of public life become magnets. We draw forth both the best and the worst within people. On the one hand we can experience the great joy of leading someone to faith in Jesus Christ or walking beside them when they discover the deep joy of discipleship. We can participate in the growth of leaders and see, more fully than most, how ministry can impact individuals, families, and communities near and far.

But on the other hand, we also become the magnets for unresolved parental and authority issues. We are the most quickly identified persons when something goes awry and the natural tendency to blame kicks in. And we are human. Some of the commitments that we make we never intended to make, and others that we intended to keep we fail to follow through on.

If the purpose is the cross and empty tomb, then we can afford to be gracious to ourselves and with others. If our purpose is other than the mission of growing God's kingdom, then we will find ourselves waylaid and distracted—stuck in activity that we know isn't moving anyone or anything forward.

We have the best theology in the world. We regularly teach and preach it to others—and withhold it from ourselves. We strive for excellence and then punish ourselves for imperfection. But excellence and perfection have never been the same thing. Disciples celebrate their imperfection as the doorway to God's grace. We repent of our shortcomings and claim the forgiveness of Christ that promises a new beginning no matter what. We keep on focus—just as Paul never lost sight of his goal of preaching in Rome.

I love to hear the stories of people who have experienced the call of God to ministry. Sometimes it has been the story of one who discovered the joy of Christian service as a volunteer in a particular ministry of the church. At other times it is the story of God calling to the ordained or full-time lay ministry. What I find fascinating is that, after the story is told, the one who tells it is strengthened. In the business of our lives, in the busy-ness of our lives, we can lose sight of God's call to each of us. No wonder we lose our sense of personal significance. When others share the story of their call, I find that they can most often refocus on what really matters to them. When we are able to spend our time and energy on what we truly believe matters, we live on purpose.

Rediscover your call. Invite a group of disciples over and share your story of God's call in your life. Then invite others to share. Then ask how the congregation serves and empowers them to live their call. Ask them how the church could more effectively be the organization that articulates God's call and then celebrates and nourishes it in the lives of our disciples.

Then watch what happens. Watch as people share, and see if you too can observe the Holy Spirit at work strengthening them, refocusing them to their purpose in this place and time. Watch what happens when they give suggestions for the church becoming the community for the calling of disciples as well as the celebrating and nourishing of each person's call.

"If you died today," the presenter asked, "how would you assess your life? Did you accomplish anything? Of what are you most proud?"

And I thought about it. I thought of the joys and challenges of ministry. I reflected on my own reluctant following of God's call into ministry. I thought of my family and the great people I think my children have become.

I also remembered some of my greatest disappointments. I thought of some of the friends I have known who have moved away. I thought of times when I moved too.

But all in all, I am grateful. God has done more for me and with me than I could ever have imagined. I hope that's true for you as well. Jesus Christ offers us abundant life. I take him at his word. I believe that the heart of God grieves for lives that are lived far below their potential. I know that the Holy Spirit is saddened by our willingness to live lives that are less than what we are worthy of.

Every day, God gives each of us the very same treasure: a new day with new possibilities. The question is: What will we do with this treasure? We cannot remake the past. We cannot determine the future. We can invest fully in today. With the power and presence of God's Holy Spirit we can look for, identify, and claim the blessings that God scatters before us. With God's help we can claim at least some of the opportunities for personal growth. And we can, through the spiritual sight of faith, catch a small glimpse of how we can influence for good the lives of others. That's a life worth our living it!

I can imagine no greater joy, no more profound purpose than being a disciple of Jesus Christ and inviting others to know him. Can you? This is the lesson of the book of Acts.

# Questions and Reflections

1. Have you experienced the power of persistence?

2. What has distracted you recently? Can you identify within yourself what it is that captures your attention or heart by the distraction?

3. Is your life on purpose? Is the ministry of your congregation on purpose? How? If not, what can you do to regain purpose for yourself or your congregation?

4. What would you wish people would say about you—not when you are dead, but now? What do you wish people would say about your congregation and its ministry? What's keeping them from saying it?